Healing
IN CHRIST'S
LIGHT

FROM PATTERNS OF SEXUAL BETRAYAL

FROM PATTERNS OF SEXUAL BETRAYAL

Jeni Brockbank

CFI
An imprint of Cedar Fort, Inc.
Springville, Utah

© 2023 Author Jeni Brockbank
Artwork © Annie Henri Nader (used with permission)
All rights reserved.

No part of this book may be reproduced in any form whatsoever, whether by graphic, visual, electronic, film, microfilm, tape recording, or any other means, without prior written permission of the publisher, except in the case of brief passages embodied in critical reviews and articles.

This is not an official publication of The Church of Jesus Christ of Latter-day Saints. The opinions and views expressed herein belong solely to the author and do not necessarily represent the opinions or views of Cedar Fort, Inc. Permission for the use of sources, graphics, and photos is also solely the responsibility of the author.

Paperback ISBN 13: 978-1-4621-4610-9
Ebook ISBN 13: 978-1-4621-4654-3

Published by CFI, an imprint of Cedar Fort, Inc.
2373 W. 700 S., Suite 100, Springville, UT 84663
Distributed by Cedar Fort, Inc., www.cedarfort.com

Library of Congress Registration Number: 2023942321

Cover design by Shawnda Craig
Cover design © 2023 Cedar Fort, Inc.
Edited and Typeset by Liz Kazandzhy

Printed in the United States of America

10 9 8 7 6 5 4 3 2 1

Printed on acid-free paper

Dedicated to my daughters Jessica, Chelsea, and Chloe and to my future granddaughters, great-granddaughters, and other posterity. May you explore tools for healing that are rooted in the doctrine of Christ. I am cheering each of you on! I love you all dearly.

Contents

Acknowledgments ix
Introduction 1

Stage 1: Searching for and Embracing Peace

1 Betrayal: A Modern-Day Plague 13
2 Finding Safety 31
3 Soul-Care 41
4 About Compulsions and Addictions 47
5 Let God Prevail 57
6 Healing the Relationships with Self and Heavenly Father 73
7 I Like Red 81

Stage 2: Grief, Mourning, and the Savior

8 The Doctrine of Boundaries 91
9 Honoring Emotions 109
10 A Commitment to the Truth .121

Stage 3: Self-Refinement

11 The Delight of Self-Refinement 131
12 Learning to Have a Voice 147
13 The Lord's Secret Weapon Is You 165

Epilogue 171
About the Author 172

Acknowledgments

I humbly give gratitude to my husband, Bart, for his support in my sharing pieces of our story publicly. I am aware that this leaves him exposed, and I appreciate his desire to help reduce shame around the subjects of sexual compulsion and addiction recovery and how it can affect family members. Bart, I think that you are incredibly courageous, and I honor your sacrifice. Thank you for being brave. I believe that many will find hope in your example. I love and appreciate you.

To my three dear "This Is Us" friends who shall remain anonymous—I am so grateful for how each of you shows up for me daily. Much of what I share is directly because you were and are willing to walk with me through the refiner's fire. Your friendship and willingness to share what you know has been priceless to me. Thank you for letting me show up imperfectly and loving me still. I count each of you among my greatest blessings, and I believe that we were friends long before our earthly meeting. I love and cherish each of you.

And to Katy Willis, I will forever be grateful that you pushed back on my ideas of how the gospel "should" look when patterns of sexual betrayal are present. Our conversations over the years have led me to seek, dig deep, and uncover precious truths, for which I am incredibly grateful. You model truth spoken with immense compassion. I am honored to continue searching for new understandings with you as my friend and mentor.

To my dear friend, Michelle. You will undoubtedly see evidence of our conversations sprinkled throughout this book. Your dive into doctrine and your ability to apply it has enriched and strengthened my understanding in amazing ways. Thanks for being the kind of friend who touches the hem of the Savior's garment and then authentically tells everyone about the amazing things He can do. I love you dearly.

I gratefully acknowledge that in and of myself, I would not have enough knowledge and support to walk this journey, let alone write a book about it. I am humbled to tears at the thought of an attentive Godhead who put many people in my path. The following individuals and programs have helped me find healing in humbling ways. It is because of countless conversations, recovery meetings, organized programs, and well-trained professionals that I have been able to seek healing and eventually write this book. Each of them has earned my gratitude and love. I am certain I have missed some people, which was in no way intentional. Listing someone's name or a program does not mean that those persons agree or disagree with me. I take full responsibility for what I have written.

(Names of individuals are used in various forms with permission and respecting confidentiality when needed.)

- The Addiction Recovery Program (ARP) via The Church of Jesus Christ of Latter-day Saints
- Aimee M.
- A. J. M.
- Alisha E.
- Allyson S.
- Anarie
- Autumn Bennett
- Bart Brockbank
- Belle
- C. Cox
- Chelsea Anne
- Chris Bennett
- Christie Powell-Hyer, LCSW
- Deborah G.
- Devin
- Dr. Kevin Skinner, LMFT, CSAT-S
- Elder and Sister Studebaker (*my* personal missionaries)
- Erin Badger
- Erin V.
- The Healing Through Christ 12-Step Program
- Jamie Lundell
- Jan
- Judy
- K. B.

- Kaelynn
- Kaitlin Thomas
- Kari A.
- Katy Willis
- KayLee Dunn, LCSW
- K. E.
- Kimberly Ann
- Kristine Payne, my mother
- Lacey H.
- L. H.
- L. S.
- Lifestar Therapy
- M. R.
- Michelle
- Mikayla S.
- Pam Blizzard, Betrayal Trauma Coach
- Rayna Callahan
- Rhyll Anne Croshaw, S.A. Lifeline
- Rob Chidester, LCSW
- Roxanne Kennedy Granata (Betrayal Trauma Coach)
- Sherie Adams Christensen, LMFT, ART, CCTP
- SJS
- Staci
- Stephen Croshaw, S.A. Lifeline
- Tara McCausland, S.A. Lifeline
- Tiffany S.
- Utah Coalition Against Pornography, UCAP

Introduction

"But I did all the things! I married a returned missionary in the temple. I diligently studied scriptures individually and with our family—daily! I faithfully gathered everyone around for home evening. I fasted often. We went to church every week. I worshiped in the temple. I prayed and prayed and *prayed* some more. This can't be my reality. It can't be. I did all the things. All of them."

This was one of many conversations I had with myself, and if I'm being honest, I still find myself digging out of internal conversations like this at times.

Nine months into our marriage, I stumbled upon evidence of pornography in our email. I thought, "This is just a lapse in judgment—just a brief mistake my husband made. No big deal. He'll confess to the bishop and that will be it."

I even remember telling him, "I love you. I forgive you. Now go talk to the bishop, and don't do it again."

But he *did* do it again.

And something wasn't right. Actually, a lot of things weren't right. He could be darling, connecting, and doting . . . until he wasn't. My husband's employment was also incredibly unstable, as was his anger and displays of hostility. And then there was the blaming me for things that weren't my fault at all.

That was so confusing. "What did I do?" I would ask myself over and over.

I tried so many things to "fix" myself and to "fix" him too:

- Sex anytime he wants? Check.
- Make sure to do all the family and couple scripture studies, prayers, and so on, in part so that he won't act out? No problem.
- Assign me as the guardian of our home and stay near my husband at all times when he's home so that he doesn't act out? Sure. I was a self-made prisoner, but if that's what it took, then I was all in.
- Keep the house calm? Well, mostly. We do have six children, but when the house was too rambunctious, he let us know in loud and intimidating ways. I obligingly tiptoed around him and was anxious for everyone else to do so as well.

So much work for so many years—seventeen and a half years to be exact, which is when we entered recovery. I was certain that all my noble efforts were keeping his sexual urges at bay and that there was no way "sex addiction" would be a problem on my watch.

That's another thing. I didn't believe in sex addiction at all back then. I just saw it as bad behavior, thinking that "addiction" was just a way to excuse it.

That is, I didn't believe in sexual addiction until . . .

I sat in shocked astonishment as I listened to my husband in our full therapeutic disclosure. I remember sinking back into my chair with wide eyes as I listened to confession after confession. Two and a half hours later and I would never be able to shut my eyes to sexual addiction again.[1]

I couldn't unsee, so to speak, and I could never go back.

The frequency of his acting out had been shocking, and none of my actions to control the situation had worked. Much to my dismay, some of my efforts to "fix" things had enabled his addiction and prolonged his delay of getting help.

Talk about a gut punch.

---

1. Note that sexual addiction is a reality in my own situation, but not all sexual acting out has roots in addiction. Some acting-out behaviors might better be classified as compulsive behaviors.

A Better Way

If all my efforts had failed, what was next? Thankfully, by that time I was already in a specialized therapy program for sexual betrayal, and I also frequented the addiction recovery program (ARP) for family members of those struggling with pornography use, which is run by The Church of Jesus Christ of Latter-day Saints.

I began to find a community of people who really got it. I started to see there were better ways to handle sexual compulsions and addictions than what I had previously employed. And thank goodness—because my efforts had backfired with alarming results.

Previously, I hadn't thought I needed my own recovery. After all, my husband was the one with the problem.

But oh, how I *did* need my own recovery! If you relate to this, dear friend, you might need your own recovery as well. I wish I could hug you.

I have used many modes for healing, such as individual therapy, marriage therapy, group therapy, trauma therapy, therapeutic yoga, meditation, 12-step programs for betrayal trauma (like Healing Through Christ and the S.A. Lifeline Foundation), many books, podcasts, and more.

I have found some benefits in all of them, and I continue to dig deep to look for Jesus in them.

I am so grateful to share with others what I have learned and continue to learn along this journey as it relates to the gospel of Jesus Christ.

Healing out loud has benefited me in breathtaking ways. I am a learner, and sharing my journey continues to be an integral part of my healing.

Who Am I to Walk with Someone through Sexual Betrayal?

For many years, I felt confused about how recovery principles correlated with the gospel of Jesus Christ. Were these principles righteous? Does doctrine back them up? Are there examples of these principles in the scriptures? As a result of these questions, I studied, applied, learned from others, and pleaded with heaven for answers. I am humbled to have been tutored by heaven, and I am also still a student who has more questions than answers.

I'm not a therapist. I am a woman who has suffered many years without the necessary tools or understanding to handle some severe circumstances. I am a mother of six, and at the time of this writing, I have been married for twenty-two years. My circumstances are extreme due to my husband's mental health issues, which can exacerbate his acting-out behaviors. This, plus the longevity of my situation and other factors, has significantly affected my own mental health.

It is tender to me that I am emerging with clarity and understanding. As someone who has been blessed to experience many modalities of healing, I'm sharing my "experiences, faith, and hope"[2] from a gospel perspective.

Your journey will look different than mine because Heavenly Father seems to delight in the creative writing process. He pens the most breathtaking individual journeys. Not everything I share will be personally tailor-made for you, but that's alright because the Lord is the most skilled custom tailor. His designs are stunning, and He can be trusted with the details. In case you need permission, I'll borrow from a common 12-step phrase: please take what you like and leave the rest.

Who am I?

I am one of you.

Why Am I Writing This Book to Women in The Church of Jesus Christ of Latter-Day Saints?

Oh, sister. I understand how hard these things are to maneuver when covenants have been made and we are striving to protect our eternal families. I misunderstood what power I had as a woman in the Church of Jesus Christ. I didn't understand that I had options, and I certainly didn't know how to use my voice to be heard and understood.

I had lots of questions: Are boundaries controlling? Is it wrong for me to feel angry? How do recovery principles fit in with the gospel of Jesus Christ?

I have sat emotionally bleeding in the offices of leaders who I thought would understand my obvious devastation, but instead I felt unintentionally missed and disregarded. I have received counsel to just forgive, without the listener understanding that in addition to my patterns of forgiveness (that were already being practiced), patterns of destructive behaviors needed interruption, and I desperately needed to know what I could and shouldn't do.

---

2. This is a common addiction recovery program phrase. See *Healing through the Savior: The Addiction Recovery Program Administration Guide*, The Church of Jesus Christ of Latter-day Saints, accessed Oct. 22, 2022, https://content.churchofjesuschrist.org/recovery/bc/recovery/ARP%20Admin%20Guide%202-28-23.28.23.pdf.

I am so grateful that there have been greater efforts to understand sexual compulsions and addictions. Hopefully, it's time to better understand the needs of the spouse and other family members. I feel called to heal with and minister to the wives of men who struggle with sexual compulsions or addictions. The severity of our circumstances can be misunderstood and often minimized, which comes from a lack of understanding and generally not malicious intent.

We're pioneers of sorts, you and I.

We need better tools for our healing and better tools to pass on to the next generation. We can become chain-breakers in this bloody war that the adversary has waged. He might have a perceived head start, but I believe this is no surprise to Heavenly Father and that He has other plans for the future. You and me? We are His secret weapons. (This book's last chapter discusses this idea more.)

Having sat in hundreds of recovery meetings, I've seen that members of the Church can have different dynamics that need a voice regarding sexual betrayal. In a way, this is my attempt to minister to my early self and to walk with those who need to hear things I yearned to understand.

I don't have all the answers, and I don't know your path, but I know the Savior does. I'm exploring and learning with you. This is a compilation of some of the things I have learned and am learning as a fellow sister recovering from patterns of sexual betrayal from a loved one. I humbly thank you and joyfully welcome you to join me on this healing journey.

It's not just you and me who need this shift and healing. Future generations can benefit from and have the opportunity to improve on such efforts. I am writing this with great love and hope for the future as we fight for our eternal families.

I wish that each of you could sit in my living room and we could share our sacred stories of pain and redemption—even if the redemption part is only in the hope stage.

Who Else Might Benefit from This Book?

Up to this point in my recovery, I have directed my outreach efforts (i.e., podcasting and social media) toward all people and all religions. Narrowing the audience I am addressing is not meant to exclude anyone, though some may feel that way. I am truly sorry if anyone feels slighted or excluded. Members of The Church of Jesus Christ of Latter-day Saints who have experienced sexual betrayal have unique challenges and sometimes feel alone, stuck, abandoned, and marginalized. Also, I love the doctrine of the restored gospel of Jesus Christ and find great joy in studying recovery principles from a Christ-centered approach. The shift in who I am reaching out to is due to the whisperings and direction of the Spirit.

Even though I am tailoring this message for members of The Church of Jesus Christ of Latter-day Saints who have experienced patterns of sexual betrayal, I welcome anyone who might need these words to join in healing. This might include people who have suffered abuse and need to understand boundaries better, those who want to learn how to use their voice in respectful and empowering ways, and those who belong to other denominations. I also welcome therapists and clergy because betrayed spouses desperately need them on our healing team.

Hope

To those who might relate to feeling betrayed, alone, stuck, abandoned, or marginalized, I offer my own experience, faith, and hope that there are better things to come. I know this much: God sees the betrayed and has great empathy for what we go through. He hears our prayers, and with Him we can learn how to better fight the plague of sexual compulsions and addictions and the resulting plague of sexual betrayal.

Whether or not any of us stay married, this journey can ignite healing in jaw-dropping ways. I have found that doors for mending hearts, minds, bodies, and spirits can open up to us in new and surprising ways when we lean into the Savior to find healing through Him. When we find individual healing through Jesus Christ, the effects ripple into our families and communities. The results can have positive, *eternal* effects. Any healing that we receive is not wasted and will benefit current and future relationships. Those who actively seek healing through the Savior speak, act, and show up differently.

Also, when both spouses choose to participate in the healing process with the Savior, the results can be stunning. Some of the marriages I most admire are those where covenants have been broken and thoroughly repaired, where both spouses have dug deep to find healing and are now thriving. In these situations, the damage caused by patterns of sexual betrayal seem to have been a catalyst for finding healing, connection, commitment, and an abiding love that is almost palpable.

For some, it is possible to yet have a "happily ever after" that is more dreamy than was previously imagined.

Compulsions, Addictions, and Other Language

Throughout this book, I use both of the words *compulsions* and *addictions*. This might seem cumbersome to some, but I consider it necessary. The word *compulsion* can minimize the severity of what some people are experiencing. Also, *addiction* is too strong of a word for other situations. I don't feel comfortable using one word or the other, and I thank you for your patience as I employ both. Please note that in my situation regarding my husband, I do use the word addiction because that is the truth for him.

Also, I strive to use language that is accessible to all.

I rarely share details of acting-out behaviors. I do, however, share some of my raw reactions.

Optional Questions and Assignments

There are several optional opportunities to answer self-reflective questions and to participate in suggested assignments. These questions and assignments are placed in text boxes to make them easy to spot, and I would encourage you to write down your answers in a separate notebook as you see fit. Science backs up the power of writing things down, and I have found this to be an important part of my own healing. Feel free to skip any such things that do not apply to you or that you prefer to not answer. There is no right or wrong answer to the questions or assignments. They are meant to help with self-awareness about ourselves and our situations.

Trauma-Informed Organization

This book is organized with a three-stage trauma model in mind. The three stages can be summarized as follows: Stage 1 establishes safety, Stage 2 honors grief and mourning, and Stage 3 integrates hard experiences into normal life.[3]

The principles in this book can work like building blocks. For instance, learning about emotional regulation is needed before learning about grief and mourning. Also, gaining a supportive community might be a critical

---

3. See Judith Herman, *Trauma and Recovery: The Aftermath of Violence—from Domestic Abuse to Political Terror* (New York: Basic Books, 1997), 155, Kindle.

step before learning to set boundaries. The three sections in this book are as follows:

- Stage 1: Searching for and Embracing Peace
- Stage 2: Grief, Mourning, and the Savior
- Stage 3: Self-Refinement

As they read, some people might uncover wounds that need to be addressed under the careful guidance of a qualified therapist. There is no need to push through healing before you're ready. I hope you feel like you have the ability to put this book down if you need more support, time, or healing before continuing. Please heal in wisdom and order.

Important Preface to Reading This Book

The Importance of Shifting

When we exercise, it's good to push ourselves. However, we don't want to pull muscles or cause other injuries. Emotional work is much the same.

The work of recovery can be heavy, and it's easy to get stuck in painful, overwhelming, and even seemingly crushing emotions. If you relate to the things I share here, then painful memories might trigger strong emotions as you read. (Sending a *big* virtual hug to those who might relate in this way.)

Learning to sit in hard emotions without being consumed by them is important. Shifting is a break from pain so that we can come back to the work of recovery from a more curious standpoint.

As you read this book, I am hopeful you will take time to pay attention to potential feelings of being overwhelmed and how those feelings are affecting you. (I am striving to pay attention to such things as I write this book.)

Shifting does not mean burying pain, nor does it mean failing to address hard things. It simply helps us shift out of overwhelming emotions so we can return to healing without being crushed.

A few things that can help me shift are doing something creative, dancing, leaning into comedy, meeting with a friend, exercising, scribbling, walking in nature, listening to music, and playing with a child. You might have different things that sing to your soul. I hope you feel empowered to search out what makes your soul sigh.

I'll discuss shifting more in chapter 9, but for now, just know that this is the general process for shifting:

1. Notice that you're feeling overwhelmed or consumed by emotion.
2. Internally say something to normalize the emotions (for example, "It makes sense that I'm feeling this way" or "I'm uncovering hard things, and it's alright that I'm struggling as I lean into this").
3. Notice what might help you shift, then do it.
4. When feeling more emotionally regulated, come back to exploring the difficult emotions with intentional curiosity. Perhaps consider a different approach, such as journaling or getting the support of a qualified professional.

Healing safely matters. I love you.

> *Are there activities you might employ to practice shifting? If so, what are they? Consider a few different activity options, such as something creative, something joyful, something relaxing, and something physical.*

The Importance of Personal Revelation

It is a deep hope of mine that you will take what works for you and custom-tailor your own path to healing with the Savior. It's more than alright if your path looks different than mine. I am not the expert on your life, but I do know who is, and He is the lover of your soul.

STAGE 1

SEARCHING FOR AND EMBRACING PEACE

Stage 1 sets up important groundwork that will be incorporated in Stage 2 and Stage 3. Please consider not skipping or minimizing the information in this first stage.

1

Betrayal: A Modern-Day Plague

The first book I read about experiencing sexual betrayal (specifically about recovering from betrayal trauma) left me with tears streaming down my face every time I picked it up. I was flooded with relief as I finally realized that I was not alone, that I was not crazy, and that help was available for my situation.

The validation was so relieving. I also felt a sense of righteous empowerment—that with further education and support, I would be able to understand what was going on with me, and that I could work with the Lord to disrupt destructive patterns that were happening in my home.

Dear sister, you aren't alone. You aren't crazy. And help is available for you as well.

If pornography is "a plague of epic proportions"[4] in our day, as Sister Joy D. Jones has said, then by default, so is sexual betrayal. (Note that pornography isn't the only way women experience sexual betrayal; it's just a common way.)

Almost 70 percent of those who receive a sexual disclosure or discovery—which includes hidden pornography use of a spouse or significant

---

4. Joy D. Jones, "Addressing Pornography: Protect, Respond, and Heal," *Ensign*, Oct. 2019.

other—suffer from severe repercussions that can include post-traumatic stress disorder (PTSD) type symptoms, often referred to as betrayal trauma.[5] Considering that one third of married men compulsively view pornography daily or weekly,[6] think about how many wives might suffer from severe mental, physical, and spiritual distress when they receive a confession or discovery. The potential numbers for those of us who are suffering are astronomical. Because most of us suffer silently, the majority of people remain unaware of this demographic.

A large factor for why we are often unnoticed is likely because spouses who suffer from sexual betrayal frequently suffer in isolation. I for one suffered alone for many years, and I have been in the sacred presence of many women who have also tried to walk the path of healing through the sludge of isolation.

I feel strongly that there should be greater awareness that many women suffer from severe side effects due to sexual betrayal and that it is more common than people think. It's important to recognize this because we can greatly improve how we approach healing and connection with those who are suffering.

With the best of intentions, suffering from the effects of sexual betrayal can be judged by ourselves and others as merely a need to forgive. Generally speaking, this is a severe minimization and misjudgment of what we are experiencing, which often includes experiencing ongoing destructive patterns and not singular events.

No one willingly chooses to face sexual betrayal. Many of us find that this particular trial hits nearly every tender and unsure part of us. Intimate betrayal can make us wonder about our identity and worth, leaving us spinning in *what ifs* and destructive thoughts like "If only I had [fill in the blank]" or "Something must be wrong with me."

---

5. See Barbara A. Steffens and Robyn L. Rennie, "The Traumatic Nature of Disclosure for Wives of Sexual Addicts," *Sexual Addiction & Compulsivity* 13 (2006):247–267. https://cdn.ymaws.com/iitap.com/resource/resmgr/arie_files/m2-traumatic-disclosure-stef.pdf

6. See Brian J. Willoughby et al., "The Porn Gap: How is Pornography Impacting Relationships between Men and Women Today?," The Wheatley Institution and the Austin Institute, 2021, https://wheatley.byu.edu/00000183-2328-dc42-a7f7-7ba86d810001/the-porn-gap.

We can suffer in tremendous ways, such as feeling crazy, feeling like we're not enough for our loved ones, and experiencing a state of compromised emotional stability. We often keep the secrets of our loved ones due to shame, fear, and a sense of devotion.

Dear sister, such experiences and reactions are normal.

Your loved one's choices to act out and betray covenants are a sign that *they* are struggling, not a sign that *you* are flawed. You are more than enough, and so am I.

Our generation is unique because, with the explosion of the internet, more of us are affected by patterns of sexual betrayal. Many more of us. I believe that our future posterity is hopeful that we will begin to break these chains so that they can have better support and healing than has been available thus far.

Your healing from sexual betrayal matters and has the potential to affect family, friends, and entire communities for generations to come. I am healing with you.

Heavenly Validation

Heaven can be very tender toward those of us who have experienced sexual betrayal.

My dear friend likes to remind me of Jacob 2:31–32, and I will pass on this balm to you as well:

> For behold, I, the Lord, have seen the sorrow, and heard the mourning of the daughters of my people in the land of Jerusalem, yea, and in all the lands of my people, because of the wickedness and abominations of their husbands.
>
> And I will not suffer, saith the Lord of Hosts, that the cries of the fair daughters of this people, which I have led out of the land of Jerusalem, shall come up unto me against the men of my people, saith the Lord of Hosts.

Does that make your soul sigh as it does mine? If so, feel free to read it again.

And then there are the Savior's words in 3 Nephi 12:28 that say, "But I say unto you, that whosoever looketh on a woman to lust after her hath committed adultery already in his heart."

Fidelity to one's spouse is so important that it's addressed in the seventh commandment: "Thou shalt not commit adultery" (Exodus 20:14).

The world might be on a path of accepting infidelity, but the Savior is the same yesterday, today, and forever, and the sexual betrayal of one's spouse, even by way of fantasy, is still not okay with Him.

Heaven has counted your tears, dear sister. You are seen, loved, and treasured. You are not alone.

> *Does it make a difference to you to learn or remember that there are commandments against infidelity and fantasy, and that the Savior has great tenderness toward those who have experienced sexual betrayal?*

THE ATONEMENT IS FOR THE BETRAYED

I once heard about a bishop who sat with a husband and wife as the husband confessed his sexual betrayal. After listening to his confession, the bishop turned to the wife and said something like "What has this been like for you?"

It melts me that she was "seen" in such a way.

Often our attention, along with the attention from professionals and priesthood leaders, is instinctually to focus attention toward the offending spouse. After all, the Atonement is for the sinner, right?

Of *course* the Atonement is for the sinner. But the Atonement is also for the heartbroken, emotionally distressed spouse.

Remember the betrayal of the Savior? "Judas, betrayest thou the Son of man with a kiss?" the Savior had asked (Luke 22:48). While this betrayal was not sexual in nature—Judas was His Apostle, and kisses were greetings—it was certainly personal. After being betrayed with a kiss, the Savior was led to events that ended at the cross.

Not only did the Savior experience betrayal regarding His death, but He also experienced what it was like to be betrayed in *your* and *my* individual situations because He suffered the Atonement. Because of this, *He can heal us.*

Christ said, "[The Father] hath sent me to heal the brokenhearted, to preach deliverance to the captives . . . and to set at liberty them that are bruised" (Luke 4:18). This verse contains validation, and it is brimming with hope as well. He can liberate us from the excruciating pain of sexual betrayal, and He can heal parts of us we didn't know needed healing. With

Him we can be set free from heartache. He understands our personal experiences better than we can because of the Atonement.

I love how Alma explains the Atonement from the aspect of suffering: "And he shall go forth, suffering pains and afflictions and temptations of every kind; and this that the word might be fulfilled which saith he will take upon him the pains and the sicknesses of his people. . . . And he will take upon him their infirmities, that his bowels may be filled with mercy, according to the flesh, that he may know according to the flesh how to succor his people according to their infirmities" (Alma 7:11–12)

Those of us who have experienced sexual betrayal can also relate to the Savior's experience of betrayal to some degree. After all, we have suffered betrayal from a loved one, and we can experience great consequences from betrayal in our circumstances.

Knowing that a God can relate to, empathize with, and ultimately heal us can be the source of hope that a broken heart needs. If you, like me, have not fully experienced this healing, just hang on. As Elder Jeffrey R. Holland said, "Some blessings come soon, some come late, some don't come until heaven—but for those who embrace the gospel of Jesus Christ, they come."[7]

Healing is possible, and each of us is worth the effort, time, and resources needed for it to occur.

> Do you believe or have hope that the Atonement can comfort the brokenhearted? Do you have hope that the Savior can heal you?

Potential Serious Effects of Experiencing Sexual Betrayal

"Hiding" in my shower with my heart racing, sweaty palms, and adrenaline plus cortisol coursing through my veins. That's where I was, even though my husband knew I had run in there, and I knew that he saw me. I felt panicked in a way I had never experienced before, and I felt like I was in mortal danger, yet I was physically safe. It was the first time I had

---

7. Jeffrey R. Holland, "An High Priest of Good Things to Come," *Ensign*, Nov. 1999, 38.

experienced an extreme "flight" response due to a discovery of acting-out behavior.

And it terrified me.

My experience may or may not be relatable because not all responses are as extreme as mine, while others are more intense. However, fight, flight, and freeze responses are not foreign to many of us whose world just imploded. They result from our brains trying to protect us when we become emotionally overloaded. In essence, the brain is saying, "You are in mortal danger!"

Quoting from excerpts from her website, Dr. Jill Manning says this about betrayal trauma:

> Betrayal trauma occurs when someone we depend on for survival, or are significantly attached to, violates our trust in a critical way. . . .
>
> Perpetrators of betrayal traumas are in close relationship with the victim, and therefore the violation of trust is experienced as a deeply personalized (versus random) offense.
>
> Due to the personalized nature of the betrayal, betrayal trauma can be more destabilizing to one's social schema than a strictly fear-based trauma. . . .
>
> Symptoms of Betrayal Trauma:
> - Anxiety
> - Hypervigilance [Constantly alert and looking for potential threats. Examples include obsessively searching through phone history, being on high alert regarding a spouse's lustful gaze while in public, etc.]
> - Feeling overwhelmed
> - Withdrawal & isolation
> - Difficulty concentrating
> - Difficulty regulating intense emotions
> - Avoidance
> - Flashbacks
> - Negative thoughts
> - Numbness & detachment
> - Sleep & appetite disturbances
> - Somatic symptoms (e.g., headaches, tremors)[8]

---

8. Jill Manning, "What Is Betrayal Trauma?," Dr. Jill Manning, accessed Feb. 17, 2023, https://drjillmanning.com/betrayal-trauma/.

If you relate to such symptoms, then you might be suffering from betrayal trauma. However, such a diagnosis would need to be made by a qualified professional.

For those who do not relate to these symptoms, then I am so glad for you. Feel free to skip through things that do not relate to your situation.

> Have you experienced, or are you experiencing now, any of the symptoms from the list above after the discovery or disclosure of your loved one's sexual acting-out behaviors? If so, which symptoms do you relate with?

You Aren't Alone: There Is Another in the Fire

Remember Shadrach, Meshach, and Abed-nego? Three young men in what should have been a deadly situation. King Nebuchadnezzar commanded their death to be by fire in a furnace so hot that it killed the mighty men who put them in.

There is no *earthly* reason that these three young men did not die as well. But God is not an earthly God.

As the king looked into the fiery furnace, he was astonished because instead of just three men, he saw a fourth who was "like the Son of God" (Daniel 3:25).

The young men were commanded to come out of that murderous inferno, and it was God's will that they were completely unharmed and without even the smell of fire on them. Their own refiner's fire had tested and proved them, and they lived to tell the tale and to continue testifying.

As wonderful as it sounds to be unharmed, that is not always the divine plan. Just ask Job, Abinadi, or Stephen.

Like Shadrach, Meshach, and Abed-nego, we do not choose the refiner's fire that we are thrown into, and it is incredibly disorienting when the person throwing us into the fire is the very one who covenanted to protect us. But just like them, we don't *ever* face it alone. Jesus is not afraid to be in the fire with us, and we do not have to walk alone.

Abiding in Christ

Christ said to Enoch, "Thou shalt abide in me, and I in you; therefore walk with me" (Moses 6: 34). Similarly, in John 15:4, He said, "Abide in me and I in you."

One meaning of the word *abide* means "to live or stay somewhere."[9] Isn't it beautiful that we can live with or stay with Christ and He with us?

I learned this lesson in a profoundly personal way a few years ago, and I share this with permission from the Spirit. At that time, we lived a few blocks from the Brigham City Utah Temple. I sometimes walked to the temple, and this particular day as I was walking, I looked down at my shoes and saw that I was wearing plain brown leather sandals. I instantly started to internally berate myself about my shoe choice. I chastised myself with internal dialogue: "Couldn't you have chosen a more appropriate shoe for the temple? Something closed-toed, maybe? Or fancier?"

As I walked while inflicting self-flagellation and paying attention to little else, I was unexpectedly interrupted by these words: "I used to wear sandals like these."

What? He's here? With me?

The shame left. Christ had offered a "me too" of sorts, and I was okay to wear brown leather sandals to the temple. After all, He once did. My heavy steps turned lighter after that experience.

Elder David A. Bednar said, "If we abide in Christ, then He will abide in and walk with us."[10] If Christ abides in us as we abide in Him, then we can have a sacred connection with Him no matter where we are. The Savior does not leave us alone in the refiner's fire. He will walk with us as we walk with Him.

We may choose to isolate ourselves from people when we experience sexual betrayal, but we are not alone. As Elder Jeffrey R. Holland tells us, "Heaven is cheering you on today, tomorrow, and forever."[11] Leading the cheering section is our precious Savior.

---

9. *Cambridge Dictionary*, s.v. "abide," accessed Oct. 19, 2022, https://dictionary.cambridge.org/us/dictionary/english/abide.
10. David A. Bednar, "But We Heeded Them Not," *Liahona*, May 2022, 16.
11. Jeffrey R. Holland, "Tomorrow the Lord Will Do Wonders among You," *Ensign* or *Liahona*, May 2016, 127.

> *Is there something about abiding in Christ that you would like to practice or try?*

Overcoming Shame on the Journey to Happiness

I stared in wonder at the women seated in our group therapy circle. They were laughing and joyful. Their circumstances were severe, and yet they could feel enough happiness to enjoy wholehearted laughter. I, on the other hand, had lost my laugh, and I couldn't seem to find it again. Their jovial moods seemed foreign to me.

I remember thinking that something was wrong with me if I couldn't feel happiness amid the agonizing experience of learning about my husband's secrets. I was shaming myself for experiencing pain that had taken my breath away. Other people also tried to pump positivity into my system, not understanding the seriousness, the shock, or the depth of what I was experiencing.

Not everyone will relate to feeling this way. However, those who do relate might feel the shock of losing joy for a time. I have some questions for you and me:

- Was Joseph Smith cheerful as he suffered severe circumstances in Liberty Jail and asked, "O God, where art thou? And where is the pavilion that covereth thy hiding place?" (Doctrine and Covenants 121:1).
- Was Job happy as he "sat down among the ashes" (Job 2:8) and cursed the day he was born due to severe losses, including the deaths of his children?
- Did Christ smile through Gethsemane and the cross when He said, "My God, my God, why hast thou forsaken me?" (Mark 15:34).

The answer to all three of these circumstances is, of course, no. *And* there's also nothing wrong with periods of heartache and mourning for you and me. Yes, we want to find joy and happiness. Christ did overcome the world, and we can again "be of good cheer" (John 16:33). But it's also okay if that's a process.

The laughter of those women did more than confuse me that day—it sparked hope as well. Maybe I won't always hurt so severely. Maybe I can find my laugh again too.

And with Christ, I did.

Take heart if you have lost your laugh or joy in your proverbial Liberty Jail. You will find it again, and the healing process can be stunning.

> Do you relate with severe overwhelm that has made joy seem far away?
>
> If you have lost joy for a time, do you have hope that it can be restored through Christ? Explain.

Healing in Community

Do you relate to offering prayers of intense desperation? The ones where your whole soul is involved, and you finally get to the point of being willing to try something—*anything*—that might help? I was praying such a prayer a few years ago. My prayer went something like this:

"Heavenly Father, I will do *anything* to improve this. I'll attend the 12-step program and ARP. I'll go to therapy. I'll read books. I can't do this on my own any longer."

As soon as those words escaped my mouth, I thought, "Wait a minute. I don't know whether it's an addiction that my husband is experiencing, but I'm praying as if it *is* an addiction." I've since decided that the revelatory part of me must have known the truth about my situation in a bone-deep way.

Up to that point, I had previously thought, "I can do this with God. He is enough." Of course He's enough, but a prompting that followed such a thought bulldozed me over: "Heavenly Father doesn't have to reinvent the wheel for you, Jeni."

The Spirit then penetrated my heart with this profound understanding that has proven true in countless ways: "I will heal you in community."

I have since learned that one of the greatest tools Heavenly Father uses to help us is His children. For many years I had not really confided in anyone, so this was a hard sell for me, and it's a hard sell for most of us. Many of us suffer in silence for years before talking to someone who can possibly help.

My first experience with talking to another woman in recovery was after my stake president suggested that I call a woman named Katy Willis. I initially rejected his suggestion, but the thought kept coming to me that I should call her.

It took me a few weeks to gain the courage to reach out, but Katy was the perfect first person to confide in. She offered genuine empathy and affirmations of "me too," and she pushed back on some of my thinking in gentle but firm ways. Katy is sunshine in human form, and my soul needed her experience, faith, and hope. That conversation marked many important things, but my favorite part was realizing this: *I am not alone.* Others can and will walk this path with me. It is possible to thrive again.

I have found that when I walk through trials with other like-minded sisters, the Savior magnifies my healing. Matthew 18:20 might offer a clue as to why that is: "For where two or three are gathered together in my name, there am I in the midst of them." Apparently, healing in such a community invites the Savior to join in those efforts, thus magnifying endeavors to find healing. Oftentimes, healing in community with others who are also seeking to mend their broken hearts is compensated in ways that aren't tangible. I can't fully articulate this gift, but I have found it to be true in my situation.

I understand that coming out of isolation can be a hard shift to make, and it might not be what everyone chooses to do. Also, I believe that the more we speak about our painful and even shameful experiences with people who take seriously their baptismal covenant to "mourn with those who mourn" (Mosiah 18:9), the more opportunities for healing we will find.

Choosing who to speak with can be a work in progress. I think it's often wise to have a gated approach when sharing tender topics, and it can go something like this: Share a little and evaluate the response. If the response is helpful and feels safe, share a little more and evaluate again. It's okay to close the gate when needed.

Here are a few questions that might help you evaluate:

- Did they lecture me?
- Are they holding me in compassion?
- Do I believe they will honor my confidentiality?
- Are they judging me unfairly?
- Is the person I am sharing this with uncomfortable?
- Do they have the emotional capacity and maturity to hear this?

When someone proves to not have capability in the area of hearing my story, I have found it helpful to recognize that it was courageous for me to try to find someone who can hold that pain and try to relate. Even when people disappoint me, heaven does not leave me alone, and I can continue to search for someone I can talk to.

There are people who get it. They are worth finding.

In meetings with other spouses who have suffered from sexual betrayal, I have felt the gentle spirit of the Savior, who seems to cradle participants in tenderness and love.

How did I ever do this alone? I have no idea, nor do I ever want to return to living in isolation.

The Sacred Walls of Recovery

Coming out of isolation is a big deal, and I can say with certainty that it is a brave thing to do.

I remember sitting in my car, drumming up the courage to walk into my first ARP family support recovery meeting. The prayer I said right before going into that meeting went something like this: "Please, oh please, oh *please* do not let anyone that I know attend this meeting!" Shame is a frequent companion when a spouse struggles with sexual compulsions or addictions.

Physical ailments most often carry much less shame. If someone has cancer, for instance, there is great compassion and empathy toward the struggling person and their family members. Dinners are brought, people visit, and other help is frequently offered. Present in such situations is an almost tangible tenderness. It seems easy to minister to someone who is physically ill.

Contrast that with emotional struggles. After sharing about sexual betrayal, we are sometimes met with stammers, silence, and judgment. It's no wonder why it's so tempting to suffer in silence when sexual betrayal lives in our homes.

Recovery looks different for everyone. For some, a basic understanding and some tools are enough, while others need more intense help. Some attend virtual meetings, while in-person connection is vital for others. Some find talk therapy to be what they need, while others might connect with a horse. (It's a thing!) Yoga can be a wonderful healing tool to help develop greater self-awareness and grow in mindfulness. So many factors make the options endless.

There is no right or wrong way to work recovery as long as God is at the center of our journey—as long as we "let God prevail,"[12] as President Russell M. Nelson has counseled.

Sometimes people have painful experiences in recovery situations, which makes it hard to want to go back. To me, it seems wise to just try something, and if it doesn't work, try something else. For instance, I've been to recovery meetings that did not feel emotionally safe, and I did not return. However, there was still a need for me to heal in community with others. Thankfully, I was able to find other meetings that better met my needs.

> What support would feel good to your soul and helpful at this time?
>
> Is there something that has held you back from finding the support that you need?

The Four A's

So often, issues in marriage are due to two people who are learning and growing. However, there are four things that should be treated as exceptions to this:

- Addiction
- Adultery
- Abuse
- Abandonment

Because this book is addressed to women who are possibly in the midst of experiencing one or more of the four A's, please be aware that not every authority figure understands this. With the best of intentions, therapists and clergy often treat such situations as "marriage issues" when such things are not the fault of the other spouse.

Well-intentioned professionals and clergy can also mistakenly validate the spouse who is participating in one or more of the 4 A's. The result can be

---

12. Russell M. Nelson, "Let God Prevail," *Ensign* or *Liahona*, Nov. 2020, 92.

that the betraying spouse can then justify and increase destructive behavior and feel more entitled. These well-intentioned yet inappropriate responses from authority figures can cause great distress and even secondary trauma. In some situations, such responses can even perpetuate an increase in abuse for the receiving spouse.

When a spouse displays any of these A-type behaviors, it's often better to focus on our own healing until the other party has changed their behavior or is at least working hard at changing that behavior.

Some therapists and clergy are striving to make marriage therapy and counseling with clergy a safer experience for betrayed spouses. However, these efforts are not yet standard and are still being developed.

For priesthood leaders, I often pray intently before counseling with them and strive to receive revelation about whether or not visiting with them is a good choice at that time. While praying about such things in my own situation, I have twice felt prompted to visit my stake president instead of my bishop, which proved to be a better choice in those situations. This might seem extreme to some, and that's alright. No answer is right or wrong if you are relying on Heavenly Father for your personal direction.

I normally don't give actual advice, but I'll break my own rule for this: If during a therapy session, due to your loved one participating in one or more of the four A's, you are asked what *your* role in their behavior is—or it is suggested that you could change X, Y, or Z about yourself to fix the behavior of your loved one—do the following three things: Thank them for their time. Slowly back away toward the door and open it. *Walk out and find another therapist should that still be a need.*

For clergy who don't understand the seriousness of the four A's, boundaries are also a good idea. This subject is discussed in greater depth in chapter 12.

Spouses who have experienced sexual betrayal do have things to work on. However, experiencing behaviors like the four A's is not the fault of the person on the receiving end, no matter what we have or have not done.

CHAPTER 1: BETRAYAL: A MODERN-DAY PLAGUE

> *In your marriage or committed relationship, have you experienced patterns of your loved one's addiction, abuse, adultery, or abandonment? If so, in what ways has that been manifested?*
>
> *If you have experienced any of the four A's from your loved one, have you sought out help? If so, what was your experience like?*

QUALIFIED THERAPY

Having spent time and money to unravel previous therapy endeavors, I hope that others can use my experience to be more cautious than I once was. It came as a shock to me that not every therapist was qualified to understand my situation. I strongly believe that therapists enter their field with a desire to help, and I also believe in their good intentions. Because our society is still studying how to best help sexually betrayed partners, we are still in the pioneering stage. This extends to therapists.

Qualified therapy can be critical for finding healing, and if you are considering seeing a therapist, I want you to know that even the consideration is incredibly brave. Having gone through a few therapists, I would like to take a little space to discuss a few tips for finding a *qualified* therapist.

I admit that I experience "therapy envy" (a phrase my cute friend Michelle uses) when I hear about things that APSATS therapists are trained to do. APSATS stands for "The Association of Partners of Sex Addicts Trauma Specialists,"[13] and they are trained to advocate for and empower the betrayed spouse in really beautiful ways. It is certainly worth looking into current availability in your area as you search for a therapist who is specifically trained to treat those who are suffering from betrayal trauma.

Another type of therapist to consider could be a CSAT therapist, which stands for "Certified Sexual Addiction Therapist." They are trained to specifically understand the addiction side of things. I have found that what a CSAT therapist understands about the experience of the betrayed partner can be hit and miss. It might be a good idea to interview a potential CSAT therapist with questions such as "What is your stance on treating trauma that is experienced by the sexually betrayed spouse?" Please note that a CSAT therapist is notably different from a sex therapist.

---

13. Visit https://www.apsats.org/ to learn more.

I found my current therapist after my friend recommended her. My friend had also shared a Utah Coalition Against Pornography (UCAP) presentation with me where my soon-to-be therapist was a presenter.[14] The things my therapist shared in that presentation resonated with me, and she has been a great guide in my healing process. Even though my therapist is neither an APSATS nor a CSAT therapist, she is still a wonderful match for my situation.

Another important consideration is that therapy is not the appropriate time to have to defend religious beliefs. Some therapists do engage in behavior that might put their clients in a position to guard their religious convictions. Those of us who are struggling with broken hearts do not need the added pressure of defending religious beliefs to therapists we hire to help us. Also, though, just because a therapist is a member of the Church doesn't mean they're qualified to handle patterns of sexual betrayal.

Family Services, which is run by The Church of Jesus Christ of Latter-day Saints, provides "short-term professional counseling."[15] Short-term time constraints do not generally allow for treatment via a trauma model, which in my personal experience can be critical for thorough healing from patterns of sexual betrayal. This is not a criticism of Family Services but simply meant to share an awareness of their business model.

Group therapy that's specific to betrayal trauma is one of my favorite modes for healing. Group therapy allows participants to realize they are not alone, allows opportunity to find community with others who understand, and is generally more affordable than individual therapy. Many areas have therapists who run such groups, and calling local therapy offices is a good idea to find one near you.

It's important to remember that therapists are not perfect—because that's not possible. They do have training that can often help us in our healing, but because they are human, they might fall short. When they offer thoughts and advice that do not feel quite right, make sure to run such

---

14. See Sherie Adams Christensen, "Betrayal Trauma, Hope and Healing: How Do I Find My Way Out?," Utah Coalition Against Pornography, Apr. 20, 2019, https://utahcoalition.org/project/sherie-adams-christensen/.

15. "Counseling Services," The Church of Jesus Christ of Latter-day Saints, accessed Oct. 3, 2022, https://providentliving.churchofjesuschrist.org/lds-family-services/counseling-services.

counsel through God. We are empowered when we trust God above all others and when we let God prevail.

> Do you think that qualified therapy might be a need in your situation? If so, do you have a qualified therapist? If not, what steps might you take to find one?

2

Finding Safety

I found myself lamenting to my therapist that I wanted to be more healed. Why, oh *why*, was I still struggling so severely? Her quick and compassionate response brought tears to my eyes: "We don't expect soldiers to heal from PTSD while they're being shot at."[16] Basically, I wasn't feeling safe and needed to first establish safety before lasting healing could occur.

If you relate to PTSD-type symptoms (such as the ones listed in chapter 1), then you likely relate to what it feels like to not feel "safe." It is common for our brains to fire messages of "DANGER!" when we have experienced patterns of not knowing what the truth is about our situation.

Many people scratch their heads when the word *safety* comes up and wonder if there is physical or sexual abuse happening. Those are definitely possibilities in some situations, but I'm talking about a lack of emotional safety—something that's a frequent experience for many of us who have loved ones struggling with sexual compulsions or addictions.

There are copious reasons why someone might not feel emotionally safe. In the case of sexual betrayal, it is very common that a loved one's compulsion or addiction has thrived in the dark. This often means that women find themselves discovering that sexual betrayal has been happening for long

---

16. Sherie Christensen, LMFT, ART, CCTP, during an individual therapy session sometime between 2021 and 2022.

periods of time, sometimes for decades even, and was previously unknown. (Raising my hand here.)

It is reasonable to expect that our spouses are honoring fidelity, and of course it is disorienting to learn that our vision of life up to that point was often not a truthful one.

Finding safety is a beautiful exploration of how to become physically, emotionally, and spiritually stable. This part of recovery can offer tremendous relief because (at least for some of us) for the first time in a long time, we get to matter. *You* get to matter.

In the next section, let's begin to explore safety by practicing being present.

> *Have you experienced feeling a lack of safety, including emotional safety, in your marriage relationship? If so, how has that manifested?*

BEING PRESENT

An important element in creating safety is to have the ability to notice what is going on with our whole soul. It's hard to find safety when we have disconnected from ourselves enough that we don't notice signals. Becoming present is a vital part of finding safety.

I have often wondered how Heavenly Father can possibly hear every prayer and be involved in so many golden threads in the lives of His children. He even says, "All things are present before me" (Doctrine and Covenants 38:2). It never ceases to amaze me that He knows the number of hairs on each of our heads (see Luke 12:7). How is that even possible? I don't know all of the ways He can do this, but I do believe He has an awe-inspiring ability to stay focused by being present.

In our mortal states, I don't believe that we yet have the capacity to have all things present before us continually as our Heavenly Father does. But we can still practice this eternal principle in smaller pieces, and doing so can help us along our eternal journeys.

Learning to be present is a critical piece of healing because it provides self-awareness and grounding. This ultimately helps us respond in appropriate and sometimes empowering ways. Recovering the ability to be present and aware are muscles we should practice using when we can.

Dissociation

A common experience for those of us who have gone through sexual betrayal is to become unaware of our bodies, emotions, and the outside world, which is often referred to as dissociation. While it is normal to dissociate when we are faced with overwhelming circumstances, long periods of dissociation can be destructive to ourselves and others. A few ways this might manifest are as follows:

- We might respond to a circumstance more strongly than is appropriate.
- It becomes easy to not be aware of our physical needs, and without that awareness, we can unintentionally neglect or overindulge those needs.
- Sometimes permanent decisions are made prematurely due to not having emotional stability.
- We can become numb for long periods of time, which can create difficulty when needing to make important decisions.

Becoming self-aware is a critical component to becoming emotionally, physically, and spiritually stable. This is because when we are aware of things that are ailing us, we can usually find ways to remedy them.

Here are a few examples of why being present is critical:

- I can become grouchy when I don't drink enough water. When I become present enough to notice this physical need, I can increase my water intake and ultimately not be as grouchy.
- When I am lonely, I can shift into depression. Recognizing signs of loneliness—such as heaviness that I feel in my chest along with a somber mood—can give me the awareness I need to find connection with someone else.
- Maybe my soul feels hungry for divine light. How relieving it can be to bring awareness to this so that I can then seek out things that will hopefully add light to my life.
- When I am outside of my window of emotional tolerance, my voice can become louder than I intend it to be. And sadly, my family can be affected by this. Becoming present can allow me to notice that my level of distress is high, and this awareness can empower me to

better meet those needs. When I do meet those needs, emotions feel more manageable.

I am ultimately a much better daughter of God when I can recognize my need to be present. I am better able to meet my needs in healthy ways and to respond with greater capacity and awareness.

Becoming self-aware by being present can be broken down into being present in our bodies, emotionally, and spiritually.

Becoming Present in Our Bodies

Becoming present in our bodies is one of the first steps to finding connection with ourselves, others, and heaven. Noticing and becoming curious about physical sensations is an important factor in this process. When we ignore things that are physically hurting us—sensations such as hunger or being full, or maybe things like your heart feeling physically heavy—we give our body a variety of messages.

One such message this could send you is that your needs don't matter. Another is that you need to prioritize *other* children of God and forget yourself completely, even though you are not well. And another possibility is that your body will start to become accustomed to you not taking care of it (but in reality will eventually compensate in ways that can harm you).

When I feel unaware of my body and its needs, I am often in a state of numbing or great distress. I will share some exercises that can help us become more present with ourselves and our needs.

One of my favorite tools is a body scan meditation. There are some free body scan meditations online, although it's something you can do on your own as well. One way I do a body scan is to bring awareness to various parts of my body by starting at my toes and slowly checking in with each part of my body as I mentally move up toward my head. This allows me to notice my body, it opens up my awareness to physically take care of myself in more conscientious ways, and it sends a message to my "temple" that it matters and is loved and cared about.

Another way to become more present in our bodies is to look for ways to engage our senses in the present moment. Consider the following:

- To engage the sense of *touch*, we might pay attention to details like shape, texture, temperature, and so on. For instance, what does the grass feel like on your bare feet? Does this rock feel smooth, bumpy,

cold, hot, or like something else? What kind of sensations do I feel when I rub a soft blanket on my face? How do socks feel on my feet? What does it feel like to run my fingers through my child's hair, or what does cold running water feel like over my wrists? If it feels safe, engaging the sense of touch can be done with your eyes closed.
- To engage the sense of *sight*, one might look for three things in a category. For instance, can you find three things that are blue? Or do you see three different geometric patterns? Maybe you can look for three things that are similar in size to a rosebud. Can you find three different shapes in the clouds?
- To engage the sense of *listening*, we might ask ourselves if we can hear the air conditioner or perhaps a car passing by. Or maybe there are sounds from a nearby television. Perhaps the ticking of a clock can be heard? Can we maybe hear children playing close by?
- To engage the sense of *taste*, it's important to recognize that the goal of tasting something is to engage this sense in a mindful way and not to eat to fill our bellies. For instance, if I put a piece of chocolate in my mouth, I might intentionally pay attention to wondering if the chocolate is smooth or rough. Are there maybe hard bumps from nuts in it? Is it sweet or perhaps bitter? How long does it take to melt in my mouth?
- To engage the sense of *smell*, some people might like to smell lotions, while others might keep essential oils on hand. It can be helpful to just notice smells in the air and to pay attention to details. For example, is the smell fruity, musky, sweet, or maybe something else?

Engaging our senses by feeling, looking, listening, tasting, and smelling can be a great way to become present in our bodies.

Sometimes I say something like this: "Dear body, I know that you are hurting. I am so sorry. It makes sense that there is pain. I love you and appreciate all that you do for me. I want to spend time taking care of you so that you can have what you need. Thank you for helping me to fulfill my mission on this earth. You are so important and valuable to me."

> *What bodily sensations do you feel in this moment? If it feels safe, you might choose to close your eyes and focus on various parts of your body, or this exercise can be performed with your eyes open.*
>
> *Can you spend a few minutes intentionally engaging each of your five senses? If it's helpful, feel free to use any of the ideas listed above. After doing this, consider again noticing what bodily sensations you feel in this moment. Has anything changed?*

Becoming Present with Emotions

Has your voice ever started to become more and more elevated without you intending to have that happen? Or maybe you are having a hard time being your normal loving self with people who have not harmed you. Does happiness ever seem beyond your reach? Maybe you don't even know what you feel at times. Do any of these seem relatable to you? Or maybe something else? I personally relate to all these feelings and more.

Each of us has our own window of tolerance, which can change depending on various circumstances. It's okay if my window of tolerance looks different than anyone else's. It is the responsibility of each individual to learn what it feels like to become emotionally regulated and unregulated because no one else can do this for us.

I once thought that emotions were not something to pay close attention to. For some reason, there has been shame attached to them for me, and I pushed them aside and carried on as best as I knew how.

Did you know that emotions are normal and experiencing them is eternal? It helped me to realize that the Savior experiences emotions. Here are a few emotions He experienced that are mentioned in the scriptures:

- Joy (see Hebrews 12:2)
- Sorrow (see Mark 14:34)
- Grief (see Isaiah 53:3)
- Anger (Because there are several scriptures about the Lord being angry, I have selected one from each major book of scripture as examples: see Psalm 85:3; John 2:13–17; 2 Nephi 19:17; Doctrine and Covenants 61:5; Moses 7:34)
- Delight (see Doctrine and Covenants 76:5)

- Compassion (see Romans 9:15)
- Empathy (see Moses 7:28; John 11:35–36)
- Agony (see Luke 22: 44)
- Jealousy (see Exodus 20:5; Mosiah 11:22)

Another side to experiencing hard emotions is that it's easy to shut off being present with emotion. Again, part of this is divinely designed, especially when emotions become overwhelming.

Also, when we consistently numb emotions, the unintentional side effect is to lose connection with emotions that are considered to be more positive, such as joy and delight. This can become particularly problematic when emotions are subdued over a long period of time.

We explore more about emotions in chapter 9. For now, it's enough to just notice what you are presently feeling.

For instance, at this moment I am feeling a large mix of emotions that include excitement, distress, relief, and anxiety, and I can feel an internal battle for peace.

> *What emotions are you feeling at this moment? Please note that this exercise is for the present moment and is not an inventory of past emotions.*

Becoming More Spiritually Present

Becoming more spiritually present can include many different things, and for me it's linked strongly to revelation. It can incorporate feelings of wonder, curiosity, and delight. Being spiritually present is not a checklist and can look different for each individual.

Some people consider being spiritually present to be more of a connection with nature. Wondering at the stars is an example of how some might become more spiritually present. Studying the details of a flower, watching the ripples on water, and noticing the texture of rocks can all remind us that we have an amazing Creator.

Meditation trains a distressed mind to be still and to observe. One of the greatest struggles with meditation can be the inability to sit still and observe. That's alright, though, because we can notice that our minds are wandering and gently bring our attention back. Sometimes minds can be trained to be still, and this can help with becoming present. President David O. McKay said, "Meditation is one of the most secret, most sacred doors through which we pass into the presence of the Lord."[17] Please note that during the initial onset of a distressing situation, meditation might be an intense struggle. I have found that being patient with myself during such times can be helpful.

For me, my ability to be present is often heightened in the temple where there are no outside distractions. Memorizing ordinances can help me to be present and focused on spiritual things when I'm in the temple while also allowing me to recall those things when I'm not there. I also find that internal conversations with heaven can be profound in the celestial room where heaven often feels near.

I like to practice being spiritually present with Heavenly Father in prayer by asking Him questions and then listening intently to His answers. Sometimes I ask Him questions that I know the answers to so that I can better understand how He is communicating with me. For instance, I might ask Him, "Do you know that my favorite color is red?" and then listen to what a "yes" answer feels like.

Other times I practice being still with my hand on my heart, which feels sacred because He formed my heart and causes it to beat. Paying attention to the sacred gift of my breath is also a way to practice being present.

> What is something you might like to practice in order to be more spiritually present?

Present Check-In

It can be helpful to regularly bring all of this together when we perform our own "Present Check-In." We might check in daily or perhaps weekly, but to do it regularly is the key. I might check in by myself, in my journal, in prayer, in group therapy, or with a friend.

Especially after hard circumstances, it takes time and practice to begin noticing where we are physically, emotionally, and spiritually in the present

---

17. *Teachings of Presidents of the Church: David O. McKay* (2011), 29.

moment, and that's okay. A Present Check-In is regarding *present* emotions and thoughts. With the awareness of a Present Check-In, we can additionally commit to things that might fill our souls and improve our state of being. It is not a time to reflect back on the past.

An example of a Present Check-In might include questions like the following:

- What emotions am I feeling?
- Where am I feeling emotions in my body in this moment?
- How is my body physically doing in this moment?
- Am I feeling spiritually connected in this moment?
- Do I have a creative activity planned for today?
- What can I specifically do to refresh my soul?
- How have I seen the hand of God in my life today?

Perhaps experiment with what your fit is for a Present Check-In. Curiosity without judgment is key, dear sister. I am practicing with you.

What questions would be helpful for you to answer during a Present Check-In?

Consider setting a goal about how often you might like to do a self check-in (for example, daily, every other day, weekly, etc.). What is your goal?

3

Soul-Care

The word *self-care* resonates with me, but it doesn't resonate with everyone and that's okay. I personally love calling it *soul-care*, which incorporates taking care of both the body and the spirit.

Doctrine and Covenants 88:15 says, "And the spirit and the body are the soul of man" (and woman).

I love what Dr. Sheri Keffer says about self-care: "I believe the idea of self-care is often misunderstood. When it comes to healing post-traumatic stress, self-care is not an indulgence; it's a necessity. Our bodies, brains and minds need help to calm down. They literally can't do it on their own."[18]

As I have searched the scriptures for references of the Lord taking care of Himself, I came across a scripture that says, "On the seventh day he rested, *and was refreshed*" (Exodus 31:17; emphasis added)

To feel refreshed and replenished is ultimately an unselfish goal because when we feel replenished, we have more to give. During times when we experience great suffering, it is often necessary to become refreshed and replenished on more than just the Sabbath day.

During His earthly ministry, there were other times when the Savior sought solitude to replenish His energy. Consider, for example, Matthew 14:23: "And when he had sent the multitudes away, he went up into a

---

18. Dr. Sheri Keffer, *Intimate Deception, Healing the Wounds of Sexual Betrayal* (Ada, MI: Revell, 2018), 278, Kindle.

mountain apart to pray: and when the evening was come, he was there alone." There's also Luke 6:12: "And it came to pass in those days, that he went out into a mountain to pray, and continued all night in prayer to God."

If the Savior can practice soul-care, then I have decided that I can as well, and you can follow in His footsteps too, dear sister.

Taking care of ourselves can seem like a selfish concept. But let's consider the temple. There is something so special about cleaning the temple for me. I have not yet cleaned the chandeliers, but did you know that each individual crystal is regularly cleaned? Vents are cleaned as well, the carpet is raked after vacuuming the celestial room (so that there aren't any lines), and surfaces that are regularly touched get sterilized. I don't think I've ever heard anyone criticize others for taking wonderful care of the temple. Careful attention is paid to the design and decoration of a temple, and temples are maintained with an amazing attention to detail.

Here's the contrast, though. Somehow, that concept can be forgotten or shamed when referring to the temple of our bodies. 1 Corinthians 3:16 says, "Know ye not that ye are the temple of God?" If our bodies are temples—and they are—then taking excellent care of them emotionally, spiritually, and physically is also a worthy endeavor.

> *What are your thoughts about soul-care?*
>
> *Is soul-care a regular and intentional practice in your life? If not, is there a form of soul-care you might be willing to try?*

Soul-Care Ideas

True soul-care requires self-awareness and might look different from day to day. To determine the best way to refresh my soul, I need to check in with myself physically, emotionally, and spiritually. Here are a few examples of how to replenish based on observations.

Physical Refreshment Ideas

- I might notice that my back is very sore. A hot bath might really help soften the muscles and can refresh my physical capacity to move more freely.
- Often, when life hits me with a figurative two-by-four, I need physical rest. Perhaps more sleep or simply not pushing through my day should be considered.
- Movement might also help elevate endorphin levels. Would exercise help, like a walk with a friend?
- Might more femininity nourish my soul? Something like painting my nails or spending extra time getting ready for the day might feel good.
- When I am not very aware of my body, yoga or meditation are both great tools to increase that awareness.
- Maybe my bedroom is cluttered and I feel overwhelmed to be in that room. It might be a great physical activity to declutter and organize.

How might you practice soul-care for your body?

Emotional Refreshment Ideas

- If I notice I am feeling isolated and lonely, I might feel refreshed by reaching out to friends to meet for a long lunch and a great chat. I might also attend a recovery meeting or have a tender conversation with my Heavenly Father when loneliness is present.
- Perhaps I am overstimulated and need to practice stillness. If so, meditation might help.
- It has, at times, filled me to create something. Seriously, I can feel my soul sigh when I create. Creating can feel physical and spiritual as well as emotional.
- Journaling can organize thoughts and emotions, much like a mess of yarn can be untangled.
- A good body cry can also help release emotional pain.

> How might you practice soul-care for your emotional well-being?

Spiritual Refreshment Ideas

- Maybe my spirit is in need of awe or solitude. Taking a walk in nature or staring at the stars might refresh my soul.
- When I am distant from heaven, spending time in prayer, the scriptures, my patriarchal blessing, or the temple might help fill that void.
- Serving can also help refresh my soul if I check in with myself and feel physically, emotionally, and spiritually able.
- I also might ask Heavenly Father intentional questions about myself and listen intently for answers.
- One of my favorite things to do for spiritual refreshment is to do an ordinance in the temple and then sit in the celestial room until my soul feels refreshed. It seems like the connection with heaven is closer in the celestial room and that my efforts to connect with heaven in the temple are noticed. For me, the least painful ordinance when I'm hurting about subjects like eternal families is the initiatory.

> How might you practice soul-care for your spiritual well-being?

Awareness of Motive Regarding Soul-Care

Any of these ways of refreshing can be used in healthy and unhealthy ways. For instance, I remember standing in my kitchen and saying to myself, "Wow! I am really hurting. Can I make dinner for someone?" The problem was that whenever I felt pain, I hid behind service. Some might exercise excessively and others might rest when that's not a current need. Using any of these tools to mask the pain is not the goal. Authentically evaluating motive is the key to choosing the best type of soul refreshment.

Heavenly Father knows what can nourish your entire soul. If you are unsure about what would feel good to your soul, maybe consider bringing that concern to Him in prayer.

Creating a Toolbox

When emotions are high, it's hard to remember that we might need to soothe our bodies, emotions, and spirits. One helpful tool can be to assemble various things into a figurative toolbox that is ready when we need it most.

A toolbox generally has several options because what may help us feel better one day might not be the best option another day. It takes some self-awareness to recognize what might help us in that moment.

Some people like digital toolboxes that they can use on the go. This might include a folder on their phone that has things such as meaningful pictures, songs, and scriptures.

Physical toolboxes are my personal favorite. I like my toolbox to be pretty, such as a hat box. Some ideas for things in a physical toolbox might include a very soft blanket, scriptures that are important to you, and pretty rocks. Other ideas are to include an heirloom from a family member, your patriarchal blessing, or some quotes that you love. More ideas include things that engage the senses, like a piece of candy, a fragrant bath bomb, or an item that is your favorite color.

Whatever your toolbox looks like, I wish you joy as you take time and care to assemble something that helps remind you that you matter and that peace is important.

Does a toolbox sound like something that might help you? What are some items you might include in it?

Assignment should you choose:
Create your own toolbox and share what you have assembled with someone who can support you in your quest for emotional stability.

4

About Compulsions and Addictions

The focus of this book is to help spouses heal from sexual betrayal. It is important that the primary focus is on our own healing. Part of that healing is a general understanding of sexual compulsions and addictions. Such education can help us have a better awareness that their struggles are not because of our shortcomings.

Shame Is the Root: Hide

In the Garden of Eden, everything was blissful until the serpent found his opportunity. Eating the forbidden fruit had opened the eyes of Adam and Eve, and the serpent's timing was impeccable as he planted the thought in their minds to *hide*.

The serpent's use of shame is still a favorite battle strategy. He encourages all of us to camouflage our actions, pain, and struggles to simply blend in. With Christ, we break through the barrier of shame. Shame is the birthplace of secrecy, which is where compulsions and addictions often hide. Secrecy is where such behaviors thrive and fester and where patterns repeat until they can spin out of control.

The hard sell for most anyone who struggles with sin is that stepping into the light is where we can receive the most healing. We can't heal what we don't acknowledge. I believe that we are healed by Christ in the light.

The Law of the Harvest

Elder Neal A. Maxwell said, "The law of the harvest is nowhere more in evidence and nowhere more relentless than in family gardens!"[19]

Let's consider the law of the harvest for a moment. When you plant peonies, peonies grow. (Unless you have my black thumb, of course . . . then nothing grows.) We don't plant peas and then grow carrots as a result.

Galatians 6:7–8 says, "Be not deceived; God is not mocked: for whatsoever a man soweth, that shall he also reap. For he that soweth to his flesh shall of the flesh reap corruption, but he that soweth to the Spirit shall of the Spirit reap life everlasting."

Consider a variety of the fruits that can be experienced when seeds of compulsive pornography use are planted:

- An inability to handle emotions in healthy ways because acting out has become a habitual unhealthy coping mechanism
- Looking at people as objects for personal gratification rather than as human beings, which often includes the treatment of their spouse (for instance, the betrayed spouse's opinion might not be considered valid because they have been dehumanized to an extent)
- A lack or decrease of humility
- Deficits in honesty, sometimes even about seemingly unimportant things
- Justification and lack of accountability for destructive behaviors
- Lack of emotional connection in important relationships
- Disconnect with God or spirituality
- A tendency to seek faults in others
- Lonely feelings in the user and those who are close to them
- Lack of ability to see people as sacred children of God
- Selfishness in regard to sexual experiences with the spouse
- Unrealistic, exaggerated, or degrading expectations of one's spouse
- Fantasizing about inappropriate actions and relationships
- Grandiose thoughts of who they are, what they can do, or what they deserve
- Shame-based thoughts of themselves

---

19. Neal A. Maxwell, "Take Especial Care of Your Family," *Ensign*, May 1994, 90.

- A preference for pornography or other acting-out behaviors instead of sexual experiences with their spouse
- Sometimes hypersexuality
- Severe physical, emotional, and spiritual repercussions for the spouse, such as symptoms of betrayal trauma, due to manipulation and other factors
- The breaking of covenants
- Escalation in acting-out behaviors, which can include increased frequency, seeking relational sex (for instance, emotional or physical affairs), seeking non-relational sex (such as prostitutes and hooking up), or doing things that push one's own moral boundaries (i.e., viewing child pornography)
- Occasional physical issues as well, such as sexual dysfunction

When compulsive pornography use is sown, what is often *not* reaped is connection, love, respect, cooperation, humility, honesty, accountability, and covenant keeping, among many other things.

There is an inherent problem, if not a crisis, when a large percentage of society uses the bodies of others purely for self-gratification and forgets to see human beings as children of God. The sacredness of humanity is lost in pornography.

I am not okay with the fruits of sexual compulsions or addictions being part of my marriage. I feel a sense of holy indignation that Heavenly Father's children, many of whom are His daughters, are being viewed and treated in degrading, objectified, and often abusive ways. We are not objects to be lusted after; we are sacred beings who are worthy of love, meaningful connection, emotional and physical intimacy, and fidelity. It is wonderful to be desired by our spouses, which is inherently different from lust. Lust is purely physical, and the motive is self-gratification. Lust sees only a body and how it can be used, whereas love sees, values, and cares about an entire soul.

What are some fruits you've seen and experienced from your loved one's patterns of sexual betrayal?

About Fantasy

As mentioned previously, the seventh commandment is to not commit adultery (see Exodus 20:14). Physical fidelity to one's spouse was the standard under the law of Moses, and during New Testament times and later, Christ included fidelity of the mind.

Fantasy is a large part of many sexual compulsions and addictions. Fantasy is harder to see because there is often no physical proof. However, it is important to understand that fantasy does play a role in acting-out behaviors, particularly when setting boundaries.

The Savior addressed the subject of inappropriate fantasies and raised the bar higher when He said, "Behold, it is written by them of old time, that thou shalt not commit adultery; But I say unto you, that whosoever looketh on a woman, to lust after her, hath committed adultery already in his heart" (3 Nephi 12:27–28).

In more recent times, the Lord also said this: "Thou shalt love thy wife with all thy heart, and shalt cleave unto her and none else. And he that looketh upon a woman to lust after her shall deny the faith, and shall not have the Spirit; and if he repents not he shall be cast out" (Doctrine and Covenants 42:22–23)

The standard set by the Savior is to have virtuous thoughts that are free from inappropriate fantasies. Covenants that are honored, nurtured, and fostered in the mind and in the heart lead to covenants that are kept physically and vice versa.

In a world that praises the objectification of God's children, expecting fidelity of the mind can be an unpopular view. It can be discouraging to stand against something that so many people praise. Virtue can be a lonely opinion these days.

The thing is, though, that we cannot change God's law. In case it's validating to hear, it's more than okay to expect thoughts and actions of fidelity from your spouse. Jesus does too.

Ranges of Pornography Use

There is a great range of intentional pornography use, which includes being occasionally curious to having a full-fledged addiction and various levels in between.

Many professionals and Church leaders discourage pornography use being classified as an "addiction," with a major concern being that labeling someone an addict will keep them stuck in patterns because of such a label.

On the other side of the spectrum is that those who struggle with actual sexual addiction can find the word "addiction" to be a safeguard of sorts. Other words tend to minimize the severity of what they've experienced, and it helps them feel a sort of caution about patterns that might repeat if they don't stay on their guard.

Range of use is subjective, and a diagnosis for actual addiction should be made by a professional.

In my own situation, it was helpful for my husband to be diagnosed with sexual addiction by a qualified professional. I needed to know the extent of my husband's relationship with pornography so that I could make more informed choices. A full therapeutic disclosure and a polygraph disclosure were both important elements in my own situation, as was SPECT brain imaging.

Even though our loved ones are struggling with addiction, it is important to remember their worth. I like how my husband sometimes introduces himself in 12-step meetings, "I'm Bart. I'm a son of God who struggles with sexual addiction." When he does this, Bart recognizes his divine identity and labels that as primarily who he is. He then labels the behavior that he is working on changing with Christ.

Regarding Pornography Addiction

A few years ago, my husband had a SPECT imaging scan performed on his brain. Before going over the results, the neurologist asked my husband if he had ever been addicted to hard drugs. The answer was no—my husband has never abused drugs or alcohol. He has, however, turned to pornography for long periods of time, and that prolonged exposure to the chemicals that pornography creates caused physical damage that looks like the results of using hard drugs.

Isn't it curios that prolonged and severe pornography use would damage his brain the same way hard drugs would?

To understand this better, it was helpful for me to learn that pornography creates chemicals in the brain. The chemicals are what the compulsion or addiction is rooted in. Acting-out behaviors are what creates the chemicals.

Dr. Donald L. Hilton queried, "Why is it that some consider adrenaline and dopamine to be drugs if drug companies produce them, yet they will not acknowledge these same chemicals to be drugs if pornography stimulates the brain to produce them?"[20]

The hard thing about combating this is that in order to access their drug of choice, one doesn't need to find a sketchy drug dealer or fabricate stories to doctors for unneeded prescriptions. They can have access most anytime on a multitude of devices or through images that are accessible in one's mind.

One common sign that compulsion has turned into a physical addiction is that withdrawals are present when they first stop acting out. One example of this occurred in my own situation after my husband had a relapse. After a few days of sobriety, I was surprised by the subsequent withdrawals he experienced. I remember feeling concerned that something was physically very wrong with him, and at one point I considered taking him to the hospital. He was at times shaking and was highly distressed. He was agitated and said things like "I feel like I'm going to crawl out of my skin" and "It feels like I'm going to die."

I was humbled that my husband let me see the inside of his sobriety journey and that he is vulnerable enough to allow me to share it with you. It helped me to see how intensely he was struggling and helped me to move toward greater empathy.

Slip versus Relapse

It can be important to recognize the difference between a slip and a relapse regarding compulsive and addictive behaviors. Professionals sometimes have differing opinions on what constitutes a slip versus a relapse. After hearing differing opinions, I will share my own understanding as it applies to my situation.

To me, a slip is a mistake that is quickly confessed to and repaired. Slips are more like bumps in the road, and while they can be painful, they are not generally as severe because there is awareness, accountability, and an interruption of the acting-out pattern.

---

20. Donald L. Hilton Jr., MD, *He Restoreth My Soul: Understanding and Breaking the Chemical and Spiritual Chains of Pornography through the Atonement of Jesus Christ* (San Antonio, TX: Forward Press Publishing, 2011), 53.

A relapse is more severe because there is a pattern involved. A relapse typically involves a lack of transparency, deceptive behaviors, and lack of accountability. Oftentimes, a relapse goes on for long periods of time. Sometimes the patterns of behavior from a relapse are eventually confessed to, or they are confessed to without a real commitment to change. Other times the behavior is discovered.

Recovery versus Sobriety

Recovery and sobriety are often misunderstood. Sobriety is about abstaining from something, while recovery is a beautiful process of healing and becoming. They also complement each other, and sobriety is a critical component of recovery. "While one can be sober without necessarily being in recovery, one cannot claim to be in recovery without sobriety."[21]

It's important to distinguish between sobriety and recovery. While sobriety can bring behavioral change, actively engaging in recovery can play an important role in a mighty change of heart. My favorite elements in someone who is living in recovery are that they strive to be humble, honest, and accountable and are willing to connect.

Evaluating the behavior of your spouse, what do their actions tell you about how they are doing with the following attributes?

Humility
Honesty
Accountability
A Willingness to Connect

About Abuse and Compulsive/Addictive Behaviors

I'm sad that a section on abuse is warranted in this book, but I consider it to be necessary because abuse is an all-too-frequent part of sexual compulsions and addictions.

---

21. *The SAL Book: Recovering Individuals, Healing Families* (Lehi, UT: S.A. Lifeline Foundation, 2021), 73.

The ARP's *Support Guide: Help for Spouses and Family of Those in Recovery* says this: "Those who suffer from compulsive behaviors sometimes participate in abusive behavior."[22] Psychological and other forms of abuse are part of my story, though I will not be expounding on that. I have also sat with many women in recovery who have shared with me their own stories of experiencing abuse of various kinds in their situations.

President Nelson strongly condemned abuse when he said:

> Let me be perfectly clear: *any* kind of abuse of women, children, or anyone is an abomination to the Lord. He grieves and *I grieve* whenever *anyone* is harmed. He mourns and *we all mourn* for each person who has fallen victim to abuse of any kind. . . . I urge each of us to be alert to anyone who might be in danger of being abused and to act promptly to protect them. The Savior will not tolerate abuse, and as His disciples, neither can we.[23]

Abusive behaviors can vary widely in relation to sexual compulsions and addictions. To briefly share, here are some of the ways that abuse can manifest when sexual compulsions/addictions are present:

1—Physical abuse is the most obvious type of abuse and can leave visible marks, bruises, abrasions, etc.

2—Psychological/emotional abuse is harder to see on the outside, but its effects can be devastating. One of the most common forms of such abuse is gaslighting, which is a more insidious form of lying because there is a motive to make the victim or target believe that there must be something wrong with them or that they are crazy. For instance, someone lying about where they went could cross over into gaslighting if they were to add lies like, "I didn't say that I was going there, you misunderstood," when they clearly did say that. Another example of emotional abuse happens when the offending person deflects and minimizes their actions by saying something like, "You're just too controlling."

3—Spiritual abuse uses beliefs to control, frighten, or manipulate another person. Spiritual abuse might look like not acting like a partnership with a spouse because of gender or priesthood authority, or twisting doctrine to justify behavior. Spiritual abuse might also employ gaslighting, making the victim or target believe that their divine worth or relationship with God is in question.

---

22. *Support Guide: Help for Spouses and Family of Those in Recovery* (2017), 54.
23. Russell M. Nelson, "What Is True?," *Liahona*, Nov. 2022, 29.

4—Financial abuse is commonly used. For instance, assets might be hidden or controlled. Family income might also be used to pay for acting out behaviors or to hide them.

5—Sexual abuse can be obvious. Sexual abuse can also include using the body of an unsuspecting spouse to act out fantasies or to fantasize about others. Sexual abuse can also include sexual exploitation such as sharing inappropriate pictures or videos of someone without their consent or filming someone without their consent. Intentionally exposing an innocent person to a sexually transmitted disease can also be termed as abusive.

6—Neglect can also be termed as abuse. Neglect in the case of sexual compulsions/addictions might look like emotional withdrawal or lack of privacy.

Sisters, abuse is not okay. If you have experienced or are experiencing abuse, I am so sorry. Please know that if abuse applies to you, you are not alone, and help is available. You are worth the time, effort, and resources to receive the necessary support to find safety and healing. Please seek qualified help.

> Have you experienced abuse as the spouse of someone who struggles with sexual compulsions or addictions? If so, what does that look like in your situation?
>
> If you have experienced abuse, what support do you need?

Mental Illness and Addiction

While those who struggle with compulsions and addictions don't usually have healthy brains, the mental illness I am addressing here is more than damage from acting out.

It wasn't until my husband and I were well into recovery that we were faced with the breathtaking fact that my husband has severe mental illness. His sexual addiction had been the focus, and we didn't understand that his addiction was a comorbidity of a very unmanageable mental state.

This was critical information, and since his diagnosis, we have been seeking out appropriate medication and specialized therapy. Learning about his mental illness has given me knowledge to respond with greater awareness regarding what I am saying and how I am saying it, which has helped tremendously.

We are still on this journey and are still seeking for more tools and understanding. For those who might suspect mental illness in their loved one, a psychological evaluation with a qualified professional is likely a good place to start.

Finding Grace for Different Schools of Thought

Some women with spouses on the less extreme side of the scale have personal experience that might lead them to believe that acting-out behaviors, particularly pornography use, is not that big of a deal and that it doesn't cause significant harm. They might view pornography use more like a blip on the road that can be worked through relatively easily.

On the other extreme can be those of us whose loved ones have more severe issues. We tend to have strong opinions about pornography use because of the calamitous destruction it has caused in our lives and the shattered families we've seen along the way.

One group can feel that judgments are harsh and people are overreacting. Others can feel desperate and disappointed that pornography use is not being taken more seriously. This wide range of different experiences can lead us to feel polarized from one another.

Because my situation is severe, I understand that I can easily fall into the latter category. I am, however, working on having a more balanced and zoomed-out view.

Might I suggest that we all take a breath and remember that we have different experiences. It's okay that there is a wide range of how acting out manifests and that the effects vary widely. Offering grace for one another and remembering that we are ultimately on the same team has the potential to create balance that can enrich conversations that might lead to better solutions.

5

Let God Prevail

President Nelson has asked, "Are *you* willing to let God prevail in your life? Are *you* willing to let God be the most important influence in your life?"[24]

I have misunderstood how to "let God prevail" as the wife of a son of God who struggles with sexual addiction. It's easy to do.

Letting God prevail is not something to "arrive" at. It is a work in progress that has layers upon layers of things to delve into. It is a topic that shifts and changes over time as we find new self-awareness and mature with God.

A side note for those who practice the 12 Steps: the concepts of "I can't," "God can," and "I will let Him" are threaded throughout the principle of letting God prevail. You will likely see threads of thoughts that are applicable to steps 1 through 3.

Let's explore.

Letting God Prevail by Keeping God at My Center

Something wasn't right. I knew that much, but I didn't know what the exact problem was. All I really knew was that things with my husband didn't make sense. He was irritated over things that confused me, and he was volatile and disconnected. It felt like I was living in a state of chaos. I decided I needed more information, so I knelt in prayer. After a process of

---

24. Russell M. Nelson, "Let God Prevail," *Ensign* or *Liahona*, Nov. 2020, 94.

intense pleading, listening, and double-checking, I knew what the problem was: pornography relapse.

We had been in recovery for a couple of years at that point, and this new understanding was incredibly disappointing. I felt desperate to avoid the painful process that would likely follow.

I approached my husband and told him about my revelatory process and the resulting understanding. My husband looked intently into my eyes and responded with sincerity that he had not been acting out. I remember pushing him for more, but in the end, I decided that I must have heard heaven incorrectly, and I decided to believe my husband. My husband's sincerity, combined with a strong desire not to go on the roller coaster of relapse, had been enough to convince me that he was telling me the truth.

As you likely guessed, I later learned that he had, indeed, relapsed.

Let's evaluate the scenario I just shared and see where I let God prevail and where I had more growing to do.

It's obvious that turning to heaven for revelation was a good choice. While checking, double-checking, and listening intently, I learned things on my knees that my eyes had not witnessed. I believed God enough to approach my husband.

Later, however, I was distracted by my husband's sincerity and by my strong desire to not have to face the pain of relapse. I wanted to believe my husband so badly that I didn't double-check his response in prayer and jumped to the conclusion that I had misheard heaven.

I started out that day letting God prevail and ended up with me and my husband prevailing. As time has fast-forwarded a few years, I have greater self-compassion for the situation that I was in, realizing that my husband's dishonesty was disorienting and emotionally abusive. It makes sense that I wanted things to be alright. This experience was a wonderful opportunity to learn that heaven does talk to me and that I am developing listening skills and am interpreting revelation.

It's so easy to let someone other than God prevail in my life. Here are a few examples of not letting God prevail in my life:

- Obsessively focusing on my husband and what he is doing
- Losing focus on what matters most

- Allowing someone else's opinion (especially authority figures such as therapists, family members, and clergy) to trump what God has told me
- Being demanding about my own needs instead of taking care of myself in healthy and humble ways

If you relate to any of these examples, I am sending you a "me too!" and a virtual hug. Of course, our responses aren't perfect at this stage of our eternal development. We are simply learning and growing, and it is naturally distressing when our marriage and families are at risk.

Learning to let God prevail holds the key to miracles, increased faith, and peace, and it's okay that this is a process. Growth is enough.

> How have you let God prevail in your situation with your loved one?
>
> Is there something you would like to improve regarding letting God prevail in your situation?

I Can't Prevail, but God Can

A critical component for recovery from sexual betrayal is to realize what we can do and what we should not do.

It can be incredibly distressing when our fairy tales are altered and sometimes even smashed by the very one who promised to keep our hearts safe. It's common to expend exhaustive efforts to stabilize the ground with elements of control. Control is often hard to see when experiencing patterns of sexual betrayal, partly because emotional safety can be severely compromised. This can lead to us feeling extreme distress and even trauma. In short, we can unintentionally have blinders on when we are emotionally compromised.

For years I strove to "repair" and please my husband, to keep my family together, and to feel stable myself. I engaged in extreme weight loss diets, tried (mostly in vain) to make our home calmer, bought lots of lingerie, and almost never said no to sex, even when he had treated me poorly. (Hmm . . . maybe *especially* when he treated me poorly because I knew that it would calm him down for a while.) I became laser-focused on what he was—and wasn't—doing. When my husband was home, so was I. I became a self-appointed guardian of my husband and our home, which ironically made me a prisoner there.

My awakening received a jolt when I walked out of our full therapeutic disclosure in a stunned daze. For the first time, I realized that my efforts had been futile and that I had unknowingly rewarded and enabled his destructive behaviors over several years. I genuinely thought I was being Christlike and that my actions were truly honorable. (I am sending myself, and anyone who might relate to this, a lot of empathy and love.)

Do you perhaps relate in your own way? Efforts to keep things stable, hold on to dreams, and keep covenants intact (that we didn't break) are rooted in beautiful intentions. When we feel like we can fix something that we have no power to repair, it gives us a false notion that we can make the outcome match our dream.

Sometimes women who have experienced sexual betrayal will intentionally view pornography in an effort to connect with their husband, compete with them, or meet their own sexual desires. I once thought about trying this method, though I am glad I never did. These thoughts were because I wondered if doing so would allow me to connect with my husband, as I was quite lonely in my marriage. Also, I wondered about the women who held my husband's attention. I was curious if I could figure out what I lacked. I erroneously wondered, If I changed myself to more closely match his fantasies, would he not look outside of our marriage for fulfillment?

Do you see the control in these lines of thinking?

I do *not* think that viewing pornography with my husband would have provided a lasting connection, nor should I compete with pornography. After all, some of the most stunning women I have ever met were within the walls of recovery, and even they could not master their husband's wandering eye. (Spoiler: that's because a spouse's choice to view pornography is not because of a deficit in us.)

Also, there is the matter of damaging my own soul should I have gone this route. Remember when Amalickiah convinced Lehonti to "come down to the foot of the mount" (Alma 47:10)? Little by little, Lehonti came down the mountain, which eventually led to Lehonti being murdered (see Alma 47:10–18). It's all too easy to let standards slide until, finally, serious sin has been committed.

We do not need to come down to the level of viewing pornography or other behaviors. "Connection" based on pornography lacks depth, encourages disrespect for humanity, and invites lust instead of love into a relationship. This is not good for individuals, nor is it helpful for a marriage.

Instead, I believe it to be a better route to invite our loved ones to join us in the search for higher ground. Such an invitation allows them to choose meaningful and rich connection—the opportunity to repair and honor covenants and view humanity as sacred.

For anyone who has gone the route of viewing pornography in an effort to connect with their spouse, I send you a lot of love and empathy. Also, I hope to offer the thought that it's alright to change direction and to seek higher ground for yourself. It's okay to change your mind.

We cannot drag our loved ones to the celestial kingdom. They have to choose it. To watch someone flounder and struggle as they decide whether or not to keep covenants can be an excruciating experience. Sometimes we prolong their hitting proverbial rocks by intervening. As my friend Michelle is fond of reminding me, we can take comfort that Christ is the actual rock.

The irony is that when we let go of our loved one, God can finally do His work. Sometimes we need to get out of heaven's way and give our loved one to God.

I can't save my loved one, but the Savior can.

> How have you tried to save your loved one?

Here is the process I used for self-compassion after I came to this realization:

- Step 1: Notice the behavior I would like to change in myself from a curious point of view.
- Step 2: Name emotions. (Looking at a feelings wheel can help.) For instance, when I realized that I had unintentionally enabled my husband's destructive behavior, I felt surprise, shame, fear, and inadequacy.
- Step 3: Self-validate and normalize that the underlying desires are normal. For me, I might say to myself, "Of course I wanted to help my husband. Anyone would want to help their spouse. I was trying to save our entire family from grief, pain, and terrible con-

sequences. My efforts were rooted in the best of intentions, and I thought that I was helping."

- Step 4: Acknowledge my new understanding and assure myself that I can practice doing things differently. In such a situation, I might say to myself, "I know more now, and I can see that my efforts to help were unintentionally harmful. I can practice breaking these patterns and can seek out the support that I need to do so." I can then gently practice new principles, and when I fall short, I can repeat the process of self-compassion.

God Can Prevail

On a memorable fast Sunday morning, I quietly said something like this in prayer: "Heavenly Father, I keep fighting for my husband in all the ways I know how. It's been a long time since I've felt loved by him, and due to his mental illness and addiction, he treats me much like an enemy. I am struggling a great deal, and I feel lonely in my marriage. You keep telling me to stay, so I stay. However, I am hungry for a loving interaction with him. Will you please help him to feel love for me and express it?"

Light filled me, and I knew that somehow He would answer my prayer. I did not tell my husband about this experience.

Later that day, as we took the sacrament, I saw and felt a visible change come over my husband. As soon as the sacrament ended, he turned to me with surprise and intensity that manifested so greatly that his face had turned red. He whispered, "I love you so deeply. I feel it in my heart and in my arms. I feel it throughout my entire body. I love you intensely."

I admit that I was so taken aback by this quick answer to my fast that astonishment produced instant tears. I received my loving interaction in a rather miraculous way. The truly wonderful thing about this experience is that it marked a change in my husband, and his behavior toward me greatly improved.

I had previously tried to explain to my husband that his behavior toward me was painful. I employed the use of boundaries, dragged him to therapy, and did many other things. None of my efforts worked, but thankfully, God is not restricted by my efforts. When I finally let go, He took over, and oh, the results were stunning!

At other times when I've let God prevail, it wasn't so beautifully packaged. Inspired in-home and out-of-home separations, for instance, were hard to follow through on at times, and the results took longer to recognize.

Yet following revelation about how to let God prevail has always been for my benefit, even if that was hard to see in such moments. Following revelation about separations, for instance, allowed me to step out of the way so that the Savior could have time with my husband. Excruciating as those periods could be, they ultimately gave my husband the opportunity to practice changing destructive patterns and to better understand what he wanted for himself, our marriage, and our family.

Others reading this might feel agony that their loved one did not choose to turn around. I am truly sorry about such experiences. In truth, I am living one day at a time, and such results could also be my reality someday. I do think that letting God prevail would look different in such situations. For instance, one might be able to face some excruciating things as their best self, with God by their side. One might also need to surrender hopes and dreams, having faith in Christ even though the outcome was not what had been hoped for. I also have a strong belief that He compensates us for such heartache.

I know this much: Jesus can do things that I simply can't. I can't explain how He does such things. *He just can.*

> Is there a burden that's too heavy for you to carry? What might you do to lay that burden at the feet of the Savior?

I Will Let God Prevail: The Power of Surrender

When I was about eight years old, I decided to test this "faith" principle I had been learning about. One night, I prayed with great intensity, asking for my entire bedroom floor to be covered in gumballs when I awoke. I closed my eyes that night, confident that I would need to clear a path to walk through my bedroom the next morning. I reasoned that my faith was strong enough for Heavenly Father to perform such a miracle. When I woke up, I remember keeping my eyes squeezed shut until I had gained the courage to open them. Needless to say, I was very disappointed.

However, a few days later, my dad quietly came into my room and handed me a pack of gum as a thoughtful gesture. My dad had never done that previously, and he hasn't done it since.

In my adult life, I've begged, pleaded, and repeatedly knocked on heaven's door for many miracles. I have found that my perceived wants and needs are sometimes viewed in heaven's eyes as more like my gumball request—not always the will of God and not always in my eternal best interest. This can be true even if it seems like my request is righteous.

Surrender is a concept that invites us to surrender our will to our Heavenly Father. It is not giving up and it is not giving in. It is choosing to see what we can change and what we can't or shouldn't change. It is honoring the agency of others.

The Savior set an example for surrender in Gethsemane when He said, "Father, if thou be willing, remove this cup from me; nevertheless not my will, but thine, be done" (Luke 22:42)

I thought I understood and lived the principle of surrender until I viewed myself under a microscope.

For example, let's take my pattern of begging Heavenly Father. The root of begging for me is often due to a feeling of desperation. In the dictionary, it gives this meaning for the word *desperation*: "loss of hope and surrender to despair" and "a state of hopelessness leading to rashness."[25]

Apparently, I'm not surrendering to His will when I beg, because I am feeling desperate (although I can offer myself some genuine self-compassion about this). One of the things I actively work on improving is to ask Heavenly Father without begging and accept whatever His answer may be.

To truly surrender to His will, it's helpful to take an honest look at what I'm feeling and to name any fear around the situation. I also need a firm understanding and faith that no matter what happens, I will be alright in the long run. True surrender comes from the humble belief that Heavenly Father has a plan and that I trust Him to implement it, even if it looks different than I had imagined. And let's face it: His plan is often different than I dreamed it to be.

When eternal covenants are at risk due to our loved one's choices, surrendering those hopes and dreams can prove to be an excruciating ordeal.

---

25. *Merriam-Webster.com Dictionary*, s.v. "desperation," accessed July 21, 2023, https://www.merriam-webster.com/dictionary/desperation.

It can feel like we are letting go of our family. When we let go of things beyond our control, we make room for the Savior to do His mighty work. Sometimes we can think we are helping when in reality we are unintentionally in heaven's way.

The result of true surrender is peace and serenity. It's an exercise in faith. It is worth the effort to practice the principle and to work it like a muscle.

A couple of scriptures seem to provide a gentle hush for my soul that helps me surrender to His will:

- "Be still and know that I am God" (Psalms 46:10).
- "Peace, be still" (Mark 4:39).

Gently hush your fears, dear one. You are in the Savior's hands.

> *Assignment should you choose:*
> *Inventory your fears by writing down things about your situation that you are afraid of. After doing this, see where faith might help with understanding. For instance, when I feel afraid that I'm not enough, I might counter such thoughts with "I am more than enough with Christ."*

Letting God Prevail by Accepting That I'm Not My Husband's Savior

Let's further consider a primary reason why controlling can be disastrous. When I use control, I am often trying to save my husband. I am trying to be his Savior. Do you perhaps relate?

I have bad news and good news for us.

The bad news is, you are not the Savior for your loved one, and therefore no amount of "fixing" yourself or anything else will cure their destructive behavior.

The good news is, you are not the Savior for your loved one, and therefore you can't fix them; however, *the Savior can* (should they become willing).

My friend Michelle reminded me of this principle when she pointed out the following scripture: "For it is expedient that there should be a great and last sacrifice; yea, not a sacrifice of man, neither of beast, neither of any manner of fowl; for it shall not be a human sacrifice; but it must be an infinite and eternal sacrifice" (Alma 34:10).

Oh, friend, you didn't *cause* it, and you can't *fix* it either. Our loved ones need an "infinite and eternal sacrifice," and we are only qualified to be a "human sacrifice." We simply can't do what the Savior can do.

Does the betrayed partner have things to work on and improve? *Yes.* Of course we do. But *also*, sexual betrayal is not our fault. There are healthy ways for our loved ones to address things that we can improve on—ways that don't include them breaking covenants. Their choice to damage trust is indeed their choice. As we learn in the second article of faith, we are not responsible for their behaviors.

My husband has a Savior, and it (thankfully) isn't me.

> How can you let go and allow space for the Savior to do His work in your situation with your loved one?

Letting God Prevail by Walking without Sight

"For we walk by faith, not by sight" (2 Corinthians 5:7).

Have you heard of someone with a physical disability having other senses heightened? For instance, someone born blind might have a stronger sense of smell, touch, or hearing. Those of us who walk in the fog of a loved one's compulsive or addictive behavior might lack sight to know exactly what our loved one is doing, but our other senses can have spiritual compensation. We are not left to wander without tools in the confusion, fog, and chaos that often accompanies acting-out behaviors.

It can feel like we are walking blind when we are not offered evidence that can be seen, heard, or touched. But our spiritual senses can be compensated in astonishing ways as we learn to purposefully and carefully tune in to the Holy Ghost. We can come to know things without physical proof because our relationship with the Holy Ghost is secure, and we come to confidently know how He is communicating with us. This can become a blessing of compensation that can help us throughout the eternities.

In 1 Nephi 12:17, we learn about mists of darkness: "And the mists of darkness are the temptations of the devil, which blindeth the eyes, and hardeneth the hearts of the children of men, and leadeth them away into broad roads, that they perish and are lost."

From my own experience, I have learned that when someone close to me is enveloped in the mists of darkness, I can often feel darkness as well. Sometimes this darkness can occur by simply being in close proximity to someone wandering off the strait and narrow path. It can also be easy to believe the lies orchestrated by the adversary, which can cause confusion. Some falsehoods include thoughts such as "This is my fault" or "If only I were _____ (thinner, more organized, more toned, etc.), this would not have happened."

While confusion, fog, and chaos are incredibly uncomfortable, they can also trigger an awareness and a remembrance that we are in the middle of a spiritual war. With this remembrance, we can evaluate with heaven how to combat such things.

Do you remember the people who were walking through the mists of darkness in the vision of the tree of life? Those who made it through the mists of darkness clung to and held fast to the iron rod, and as you know, "the iron rod is the word of God."[26] (Did you sing that phrase in your mind like I did?)

Scriptures are the obvious iron rod. Sometimes scriptures might seem to leap off the page and into our hearts. Let's consider where else we can access the word of God to expand our vision. For instance, He might whisper His words in incredibly personal ways while we're praying or even in our everyday circumstances. Words from modern-day prophets and apostles can also pierce our hearts. Listening with intent while in the temple can help us better hear messages that are meant for our hearts. The word of God can incorporate many vast sources.

It's important to know this because when we hold fast to the iron rod, it leads to the tree of life, and the tree of life represents the Savior. The word of God *is* the way to Christ. When we hold fast to it, we are not lost to the mist, even though we can't always physically see where we are going. Our focus is on Christ, and we move forward through these hard challenges by holding on to God's sacred and inspired words.

---

26. "The Iron Rod," *Hymns*, no. 274.

Letting God Prevail by Learning How Heaven Speaks to You

Even on my deathbed, I still plan on learning more about revelation and how the Lord speaks to me personally. Whenever I think that I've figured out how heaven speaks to me, I inevitably learn something new about divine communication in my personal situation.

Several years ago, I had petitioned Heavenly Father for a blessing in my marriage. I will keep the details of my request private. However, I will share that I came to know what a "heck no" response felt like from Heavenly Father. As soon as the words escaped my mouth, I found myself on my bathroom floor in shocking distress and agony. I felt sick to my stomach, there was darkness, and I was a sobbing disaster.

This event was unforgettable, and though it was deeply distressing, it led me to seek more insights regarding the severe state of my marriage.

In that instance, I learned in a real way that the Holy Ghost is not always warm and fuzzy. He also warns, and those warnings are not always very pleasant. This was a shock to my system but also a good thing to learn.

Sometimes the Holy Ghost does speak to me in warm and fuzzy ways. Sometimes He has communicated with me in dreams. I love when He guides me to a specific scripture that's so personal that I know that heaven is involved in the details of my life.

Recently, I have found that holding an internal conversation with the Lord as I take the sacrament has been a source of divine direction. I also hear heaven with much greater clarity after sitting in the celestial room for a while.

The lovely thing is that the Holy Ghost can use new ways to communicate with us. I look forward to continuing to discover how He speaks to me, as it is a thrilling journey.

Can you remember the details about a time when heaven spoke to you? What was it like? Are there patterns in how the Spirit communicates with you? If you don't yet know, or are like me and are continuing to learn, that's okay. I have found that Heavenly Father loves when I am curious about spiritual things, and He delights in manifesting Himself in various ways to His children. Consistent effort is eventually blessed.

2 Nephi 31:3 says, "For the Lord God giveth light unto the understanding; for he speaketh unto men *according to their language, unto their understanding*" (emphasis added).

Not only is He willing to communicate with me in my own language, but He communicates in a way that I will personally understand. He fluently speaks the language of Jeni, and He fluently speaks your language as well.

Elder Dale G. Renlund said, "I invite you to have the confidence to claim personal revelation for yourself, understanding what God has revealed, consistent with the scriptures and the commandments He has given through His appointed prophets and within your own purview and agency."[27]

> What are some ways heaven speaks to you?
>
> <u>Assignment should you choose:</u>
> Ask Heavenly Father to help you understand how the Holy Ghost communicates with you.

Letting God Prevail by Understanding Revelation and the Body

Do you relate to that heavy pit in your stomach that just knows something? Without physical evidence, sometimes bodies know things that our minds don't—at least not yet. This phenomenon has stunned me on multiple occasions.

A common phrase that we hear in society is "Trust your gut!" I used to think, "What does that even mean?" In my understanding, it seemed like I was expected to rely on myself instead of God. And yet . . . how did my "gut" know something that my mind had yet to register?

In response to my muddled thoughts on the matter, I pondered, studied, and experimented.

I was relieved to learn that there are scriptures that teach sacred doctrine about revelation and the body.

---

27. Dale G. Renlund, "A Framework for Personal Revelation," *Liahona*, Nov. 2022, 18.

Consider Hebrews 4:12: "For the word of God is quick, and powerful, and sharper than a two-edged sword, piercing even to the dividing asunder of *soul and spirit*, and of the *joints and marrow*, and is a discerner of the *thoughts and intents of the heart*" (emphasis added).

I also love that in Doctrine and Covenants 8:2, we learn that the body is connected to revelation: "I will tell you in your mind and in your heart, by the Holy Ghost, which shall come upon you and which shall dwell in your heart."

According to this scripture, my body follows the rule of witnesses and can provide at least two witnesses: my heart and my mind. For me, when my heart and mind become united, I have an answer. I also feel peace in both areas of my body and sometimes even see light, which for me is a third witness.

It's not all warm and fuzzy though. Sometimes warnings are uncomfortable.

One such witness that I experienced was late one night while I laid next to my husband in our bed, doing my very best to fall asleep. After quite some time of slumber eluding me, I became curious and decided to pay attention to my body. I noticed that my legs felt tight, I was hugging my side of the bed, and my chest was tight. Interesting. My body did not feel safe. I finally spoke aloud and said to my husband, "I can tell that my body doesn't feel safe. Is there anything you would like to tell me?" He replied that he didn't think there was anything he needed to tell me. After a few more minutes of silence, he finally said, "Actually, I was laying here contemplating acting out."

I came to see that my body knew that something was wrong, and it knew because of revelation.

Consider the definition of *intuition* in the dictionary: "(knowledge from) an ability to understand or know something immediately based on your feelings rather than facts."[28]

With the understanding that intuition is based on feelings, and that a primary source for receiving revelation is feelings, intuition begins to lose its mystery. Sometimes my bones just know something. Sometimes my "gut" has an understanding that my brain has yet to discover.

---

28. *Cambridge Dictionary*, s.v. "intuition," accessed Oct. 19, 2022, https://dictionary.cambridge.org/us/dictionary/english/intuition.

Also, feelings can sometimes be wrong, so it's always a good idea to double-check such things in prayer.

Sometimes this world is dark. It just is. The darkness is not necessarily a sign that we are doing anything wrong. Revelation is the way through that darkness.

> Have you yet noticed the role that your body plays in receiving revelation?
>
> <u>Assignment should you choose:</u>
> Read Doctrine and Covenants 8:2–3. Then practice asking Heavenly Father questions while paying attention to the principles taught in those scriptures.

6

Healing the Relationships with Self and Heavenly Father

Often, those of us who experience sexual betrayal come to feel that our relationship with ourselves has been significantly damaged. This is for a wide variety of reasons. Perhaps we wonder how we missed or minimized red flags, and now we have lost confidence in our own internal voice. Maybe we believed destructive lies, such as the feeling that we're not enough. Or maybe we've been the figurative "glue" for our family and have not been replenished physically, emotionally, and spiritually.

Were there times when you felt like something was off but disregarded it, and you are now not sure that you can trust yourself? I certainly relate with that. The more I rebuild trust with myself and my ability to receive and act on revelation, the more internal confidence I build.

Restoring and often improving on the relationship to self can be a critical first step to healing. This takes time and can be a process. I am still working on this aspect of my healing five years into recovery.

Building a relationship with self increases the ability to build relationships with others, including God.

> *Do you feel like your relationship with yourself has been damaged due to being in a relationship with someone participating in destructive behaviors?*

The Importance of Why

One memorable Sunday morning, I found myself tearfully on my knees with strong feelings of shame. I hated my blaring imperfections, my jealousies, my strong reactions. I considered my heart to be flawed and was very busy shaming myself about a situation in which I had not been my best self.

I was doing my best to convince Heavenly Father that I was a complete mess. As I pleaded for forgiveness and a mighty change of heart, I was surprised by the response I received. I felt like I should look at a feelings wheel, which helps with identifying both core and secondary emotions.

I found it interesting that when I identified the secondary emotions that I was experiencing, they were all in the core category of "fear." Then came the whisper that calmed my soul: "Fear not."

This fascinated me. Heavenly Father saw my less-than-perfect behavior and was showing me *why* I was behaving in such ways.

Was it possible that He was offering me empathy and compassion in the midst of my imperfections? Did He love me still, even though I am truly flawed? Yes, it is possible, and yes, He does love me despite my imperfections. One of the main reasons for this is that He understands better than I do why I am struggling.

Through this exchange, I realized Heavenly Father knew why I was hurting, and this was a catalyst that ultimately helped me to make lasting changes. Shaming myself had not previously proved helpful, but divine compassion did.

Self-Compassion

I've reflected on the compassion that Heavenly Father gifted me during my divine exchange that was shared in the previous section. I have wondered, What if I can offer myself that same compassion that was offered by heaven so that I can access it when I need it? I have since learned that I can.

I once feared self-compassion for various reasons. We can fear that we won't change if we are gentle with ourselves. We can fear that compassion might enable behavior that we want to change. We can even reason that we deserve more harshness, and the void of self-compassion becomes self-flagellation.

In reality, true self-compassion can lower shame and can help take fear out of the need to repair and change. Those who regularly practice self-compassion will likely find that their hearts are softer, there is less judgment for self and others, and there is a recognition that we all struggle sometimes.

We *might* be able to shame ourselves into better behavior, but even if we do so, we miss a rich experience that can facilitate a deeper understanding of who we are, why we are struggling to begin with, and how much we are adored by our Heavenly Father. Self-compassion bridges the gap from mistake to healing while maintaining kindness for oneself and others.

Self-compassion is infinitely more fulfilling and secure than self-esteem because it is not based on accomplishment or physical appearance. To borrow from a popular recovery phrase, I am a "human being instead of a human doing." Self-compassion allows a person to see their flaws more as the Savior does. He not only sees where we can fall short, but He also sees *why* we are falling short. I am relieved to find out that He still loves me, even though I have many imperfections.

The Pattern for Practicing Self-Compassion

There are various techniques, tips, and formulas for practicing self-compassion. As mentioned in the previous chapter, the following process is my own best fit:

- Step 1: Notice behavior that I would like to change from a curious point of view.
- Step 2: Name emotions that are being experienced. (Looking at a feelings wheel can help.)
- Step 3: Self-validate and normalize suffering.
- Step 4: Repair and gently practice change.

To use a personal example, I will refer to a time when I recognized that my voice was elevated and distressed as I spoke to my children:

- Step 1: Notice that my voice is elevated and distressed while staying curious about what is going on with me.
- Step 2: Name the emotions I am feeling: overwhelmed, tired, worried, ignored, powerless.

- Step 3: Acknowledge why I am suffering. I might say, "It makes sense that I am feeling those things. I stayed up late with a sick child, there are some heavy things on my plate, and my children do seem to be ignoring me."
- Step 4: With this new awareness, look at what I can do to remedy the situation both now and in the future. For now, I can apologize to my children for raising my voice in a distressed way. I can also see that my body might need rest and go into another room. I can also set a boundary with my children. In the future, I can practice being aware of my emotions and taking care of my needs before escalating and responding more strongly than I would prefer.

Self-compassion pays off in dividends because when we can learn to be compassionate with ourselves, we can further develop compassion for others. Like the second great commandment says, "Thou shalt love thy neighbor *as thyself*" (Mathew 12: 39; emphasis added). My capacity to love myself directly affects my capacity to love others.

Assignment should you choose:
Sometime this week, intentionally practice the four steps of self-compassion when you see a personal behavior that you would like to change. Then record your experience here:

Step 1: While staying curious, what behavior would you like to change?

Step 2: Name emotions that you're experiencing. (Looking at a feelings wheel on the internet can help.)

Step 3: Self-validate and normalize your suffering.

Step 4: Record how you plan to repair and gently practice change. Then implement it.

After practicing self-compassion, consider comparing and contrasting previous experiences with repair and change.

Chapter 6: Healing the Relationships with Self and Heavenly Father

Honoring Yourself and Facing Self-Betrayal

One of the main reasons many betrayed spouses experience a rift in the relationship with ourselves is that we come to realize we unintentionally betrayed ourselves at times. This might look like ignoring gut intuition, participating in relationships more fully than is warranted, and blaming ourselves for things that aren't our fault.

Self-betrayal can feel noble because it often requires great personal sacrifice. However, we can lose balance in this process and can eventually lose ourselves.

Shifting self-betrayal behaviors can be surprisingly difficult for many of us, and that's alright. One of my favorite aspects of 12-step work is to make amends, and one of the people we can choose to make amends with is *ourselves*. Isn't that beautiful?

A few ways we can choose to make amends with ourselves include the following:

- Spending money on needed therapy or soul-care
- Listening to our inner voices and respecting what they say
- Sharing our stories with safe people instead of living in isolation
- Setting a boundary when needed
- Offering ourselves self-compassion when we are hurting
- Not participating in things that make us feel uncomfortable
- Choosing which restaurant we would like to eat at sometimes instead of continually capitulating to the desires of others
- Developing a talent
- Resting when needed
- Taking better care of our bodies
- Spending time doing spiritual things that fill our buckets
- Loving and appreciating our bodies, even in their imperfect states

Honoring ourselves is a process and requires us to be balanced in our approach. We can still serve others while recognizing that we are also children of God who are deserving of time, effort, and resources.

> What has self-betrayal looked like in your situation?
>
> In what ways might you like to make amends to yourself?

Healing Your Relationship with God

If healing with heaven brings pain for some reason, you are not alone. Having sat in hundreds of recovery meetings with many women who have experienced genuine spiritual trauma, I want to validate that this can be incredibly distressing and that you aren't alone.

For those who need to hear this: It makes sense that some might feel betrayed by God. It makes sense that this can make healing with God painful. It makes sense that this hurts. Such feelings just make so much sense, dear sister.

Remember when Job was distressed over the magnitude of his losses? During that period of intense mourning and anguish, Job reminded the Lord of his diligence, his integrity, and his commitment to fidelity, among other things (see Job 27:5; 31:1, 19–21). He also told the Lord about his conclusions.

I think it's easy to judge Job as forgetting his faith with his line of reasoning. There's another possibility though.

I have come to believe that Job had questions regarding things that didn't make sense to him, and as he hurt intensely, he went straight to the Savior for answers. Both Job and the Savior worked through relationship issues and developed a closer relationship with one another because Job was willing to approach the Lord, ask questions, and ultimately have faith in the Lord's response. Job came to know the Savior with greater depth, which eventually led to Job seeing Him (see Job 42:5).

I've decided that this was brave of Job and that I can be brave too. When I approach heavenly beings with the perspective of developing a relationship, I am also rewarded with greater depth.

I remember praying something like this: "I'm hurting. I have done all of the right things to have an eternal family. You told me that it would be alright to marry my husband before I did so. Things are not alright, and even though I trust you, it feels like a betrayal."

Heaven's response? "Finally." As I have reflected with some confusion on this response, I realized that Heavenly Father was grateful for my honesty about what I was feeling because He could work with that. When I wasn't being emotionally honest with Him, I didn't even acknowledge that there was something to heal.

CHAPTER 6: HEALING THE RELATIONSHIPS WITH SELF AND HEAVENLY FATHER

In my own experience, I have found Heavenly Father to be so tender with me when I bring my concerns about my relationship with Him *to* Him. When I am vulnerable about how I am hurting in my relationship with Him, He has sometimes offered more clarity. Other times I have felt empathy from Him, and He has consistently stayed with me.

For me, rigorous honesty with what I'm feeling and where I'm at seems to be key. When I tell Him such things, I sometimes get the impression that He's saying something like "I am so glad you are admitting that there's a problem! Now we can work to heal this."

When I am struggling and yet pretend that all is well in my relationship with Heavenly Father, or fear telling Him what my painful emotions regarding Him are, then healing is much harder to find. Looking back, I have floundered in such places.

Being honest about emotions can be scary, but I believe that the Lord values honesty. I also believe that "the Lord loves effort,"[29] as President Nelson teaches. Efforts to find healing in divine relationships will eventually be blessed.

> Being honest with yourself, is there something you might like to work through regarding your relationship with your Heavenly Father? If so, what?
>
> Considering possible new insights, is there a new way that you might like to approach Heavenly Father to heal your relationship?

---

29. Russell M. Nelson, in Joy D. Jones, "An Especially Noble Calling," *Ensign* or *Liahona*, May 2020, 16.

7

I Like Red

Have you ever found yourself so distressed that you just wanted to sit down exactly where you were and sob? That's the state I found myself in while standing near the used nightgowns in a second-hand store a few years ago.

How did I get there? Let's rewind.

With great effort earlier that day, I had prepared my husband's dinner and then drove thirty minutes to his work. I had wanted to spend time with him and to serve him. He was not in a healthy frame of mind this particular evening, and as a result, he treated me pretty terribly. As I drove home, the emotional pain increased with each mile, and by the time I was nearly home, I realized I was an emotional mess. I knew this much: I didn't want to face my six children in such a state. So I decided that I would first stop at the Deseret Industries second-hand store that was about a block away from my home. I didn't have anything to buy, but I needed a diversion and hoped that a little extra time would help my emotional state.

As I walked through the store, I started to feel like I was wearing lead shoes. Finally, I stopped walking and found myself near the section of nightgowns. At this point, my self-made shoulder angels started to whisper their opinions.

Shoulder Angel #1: "I can't take another step. My feet won't move, my eyes are hot with tears, and my heart aches in ways I didn't know were possible. I'm going to plop down right here in the aisle by these used nightgowns and bawl my eyes out."

Shoulder Angel #2: "You can't sit down in a second-hand store and cry! People will think you're crazy!"

After internally deliberating, I flicked Shoulder Angel #1 away. I decided to pray for help, and my frozen feet were able to take one step . . . and then another. As soon as I moved, I had such a random thought come to me that I knew that it was not my own, and it was this:

"I like red."

Bewildered by this inspired change of topic, I was first stunned, then I felt seen, and I finally decided to go with it. I thought, "I *do* like red! And I prefer gold over silver. I like moody colors more than neutrals . . . and that's okay!"

When this sunk in, the reality that I had forgotten something as basic as my favorite color hit me pretty hard. How had that happened? How had I lost myself so profoundly in the name of trying to save my marriage and my family?

That day I became so incredibly determined to find something red that I walked up and down aisles with my eyes focused on anything with a vibrant apple hue. Such stores are hit-and-miss for the perfect treasure, though, and I didn't see many red items that appealed to me that day, but I was determined not to leave that store empty-handed. I ended up purchasing an unremarkable red undershirt, and when I wore that undershirt in the coming days, I again remembered that I love red.

My heart sang as I learned this: *my favorite color matters to God.*

So does yours, dear sister.

What is your favorite color and why?

Salt of the Earth

We were each created with divine design in mind—an individual masterpiece. Heaven broke the mold after you were dreamed up and created.

We were made to be a city shining on a hill! We were created to have light and individuality and to use our respective talents and gifts to be a delight and benefit to us, our fellow beings, and our God.

"Ye are the salt of the earth; but if the salt have lost his savour, wherewith shall it be salted? It is thenceforth good for nothing, but to be cast out, and to be trodden under foot of men" (Matthew 5:13).

Trodden under foot of men. During the days when my favorite color didn't seem to matter, I often referred to myself as a doormat. Doormats are used to wipe dirt and mud off of the feet of . . . well, everyone. I was often trodden under the foot of men, so to speak. Ouch.

Being reminded of my favorite color was a beginning to finding myself again. What I have to offer the world is divinely inspired, individually important, and even sacred. The same is true for you, dear sister.

Redemptive to the concept that I had started to resemble flavorless salt is that human beings differ from salt because we *can* find our flavor again if it's lost. With God, we can figure out how to be a beautiful and shining city on a hill. Our contributions can salt the earth, which in turn points ourselves and others to the light of the Savior. By exploring who we were created to be, we learn that somehow our individuality matters to Heavenly Father.

It's okay to shine, especially when we credit the source of the light. We serve our God best when we find out who He made us to be. Talents, skills, likes and dislikes, spiritual gifts, and more all serve to testify of our divine nature and that each of us has beautiful things we can contribute to ourselves, our families, our communities, and the kingdom of God.

If you could eat anything for dinner tonight, what would you choose?

What spiritual gifts are mentioned in your patriarchal blessing?

Do you consider yourself to be of great worth? Where are you at on that journey? No answer is right or wrong.

Have you asked God recently if He will tell you what He thinks of you? If not, does that feel like a helpful thing to possibly explore?

Is there a hobby or talent that you might like to develop?

Would the knowledge that your likes and dislikes are important to God have an influence on aspects of your life like wardrobe, decorating, and how you spend your time? Why or why not?

Humility and Worth

I have felt confused about how I could be a bright city that is shining on a hill while being humble. How does that work? I felt like a fish out of water when I'd consider it.

After several conversations and learning more about humility, I finally settled on this personal understanding: Humility is standing still in the sacred truth of what is, and being curious about what could be, while acknowledging the giver of all things. Humility does not puff up, nor does it shrink.

In other words, I believe that humility is a feeling of authentic accuracy in who I was created to be, while acknowledging with awe and wonder that all that I am is because of my gracious God. Humility brings curiosity, wonder, gratitude, and sacred worth.

Humility is not being timid, but it is being aware of what I say, and how I say things also matters immensely. While being humble, I can be fearless, brave, and vocal.

Here is the beautiful irony of humility: "Humble yourselves in the sight of the Lord, and he shall lift you up" (James 4: 10).

> *Do you believe you can be humble while still acknowledging your positive attributes?*

Why Your Favorite Color Matters

I have always known I was a daughter of God. What I didn't know was how a daughter of God should be treated.

Internalizing that I was created to be a city on a hill provided that first spark, which eventually lit up my entire life in amazing ways. I have found that coming to know who I am to God and how I should be treated has ignited individual worth, goals, boundaries, righteous empowerment, finding my voice, and more.

Sacred self-discovery may mature and change over time as we grow, become, and develop. The voyage can take twists and turns and can be adventurous. I have decided that it is best to explore who I am while holding on to the Savior's hand.

When we come to better understand who we are to Heavenly Father and how He wants His daughters to be treated, we do things differently.

This much I know: Heavenly Father cares about my favorite color, and He cares about such details that relate to you as well. Who we are, what we like, our hopes and dreams, and so on are important in the eternal realms. Christ delights in helping us on the path of soul discovery. Developing talents and traits is part of learning who we are and why we are here, and it ultimately helps us find a great sense of belonging and joy in His kingdom.

Worth Is Different than Worthiness

Sheri Dew taught, "None of us come to this earth to *gain* our worth; we brought it with us."[30]

The lie I told myself was that because my husband was interested in other women whom I didn't resemble, there was something wrong with me. My perceived worth was in question. It's easy to dive down such rabbit holes when we are trying to figure out *why* something happened. The underlying concept is that if we can figure out why, then we think we can fix it.

Eternally, our worth is solid. No matter what.

College degrees, children serving missions, and the "right" number on the scale can lead to false conclusions that we are worth more. Conversely, things like financial challenges, sin, and experiencing sexual betrayal can lead to equally false conclusions that we are worth less. Neither conclusion is correct.

We don't have to "hustle" for our worth. As the common saying goes, you are a human being, not a human doing.

What would it be like to just rest in God, knowing that He loves you as you are? I'm imagining that for myself as well and can tell I have work to do in that area.

Worthiness, on the other hand, is based on action and non-action. For instance, to enter the temple, we need to qualify for a temple recommend. Other standards apply to entering the waters of baptism and yet another set to being in the presence of God. In the world, someone might need a college degree and certain work experience to qualify for a specific career. These represent boundaries of sorts.

---

30. Sheri Dew, *No One Can Take Your Place* (Salt Lake City, UT: Deseret Book, 2004), 21.

For me, I strive to be better every day, and I cannot yet achieve perfection. That's okay. I am not my sins, nor am I my accomplishments. I am Jeni, a daughter of God. And with Christ, I am absolutely *more* than enough.

With Christ, you are *more* than enough as well, dear friend. Perfection is not required to increase your worth.

> Do you believe your worth is secure with the Savior and Heavenly Father? Why or why not?

Stage 2

Grief, Mourning, and the Savior

8

The Doctrine of Boundaries

I recently listened to my dear friend describe how she was being treated in emotionally abusive ways. I related to her experiences and felt protective of her. I shared my own experience regarding boundaries and felt concerned for her as she pushed back on the concept.

It was like looking in a mirror of myself a few years ago because I previously bristled at the concept of boundaries as well.

Being distressed at my friend's situation, I began praying intently for her heart to be open to the concept of boundaries so that she could have safety. The Spirit then reminded me that there are often some important building blocks that need to be in place before setting boundaries.

For example, one such building block is an understanding of our divine identity as daughters of God *and* how a daughter of God should be treated. Another building block is that of a supportive community because boundaries can be a confusing concept that can also be scary to implement.

It is wisdom to do things in order, "line upon line and precept upon precept" (2 Nephi 28:30). Previous chapters in this book help set up the necessary groundwork for boundaries.

> What support might you need to seek out before implementing boundaries?

The Doctrine of Boundaries

Boundary schmoundary, I used to think. I was decidedly against boundaries for more than seventeen years. (Or so I thought.) They seemed controlling and harsh. Wasn't it Christlike to just take things? Wasn't the Savior a martyr? Shouldn't I willingly be a martyr as well? And what does it mean to turn the other cheek?

In all actuality, my "just taking things" had turned me into a doormat and not really a martyr. (This realization took away the majesty of that concept with a clean blow to my ego.) Yes, even with noble intentions, I had become more like an object that people wiped their mud-laden shoes on. My doormat status had not helped my husband make better choices as I had hoped, and my husband had continued to participate in his addiction and poor behavior for a very long time.

My change of heart regarding boundaries came when the Spirit pierced my heart while sitting in an ARP family support meeting with this message: God uses boundaries. I remember the hope that hit me in that moment, and I concluded that day that if God uses boundaries, so can I. I'm all in now.

> How do you currently feel about boundaries? No answer is right or wrong.

What Is a Boundary?

Boundaries allow us to choose when physical, emotional, and spiritual connection with someone is a good idea or not. Boundaries can protect us from experiencing patterns of destructive behavior.

Rhyll Croshaw, co-founder of the S.A. Lifeline Foundation, said, "God sets boundaries: they are called commandments. They are for our safety and well-being. He gives them to us for our protection because He loves us. They are not to punish us but to invite us to come closer to Him. In that same manner, as we set boundaries, we invite others close and as a result, foster more intimate relationships. It is a wonderful paradox!"[31]

Boundaries act as a gate of sorts. We get to decide when to open the gate, how wide to open it, and when it needs to close again.

---

31. Rhyll Anne Croshaw, *What Can I Do About Me?* (San Antonio, TX: Forward Press Publishing, 2012), 965–6, Kindle.

Chapter 8: The Doctrine of Boundaries

While it's a nice bonus if our boundaries act as a catalyst for our loved ones to make better choices, boundaries should not be made to control anyone. Boundaries should be made based on safety and should honor agency.

> *Can you think of a boundary that God uses?*

Boundaries Are Brave

I remember the first time that I set the boundary of an in-home separation with my husband. I was terrified. Questions plagued me: What if he decides to move toward divorce? What if he has an affair because I am not being sexual with him? What if he chooses addiction over our family?

The thing was, I set the boundary of an in-home separation after consulting with God. It was needed. The problem became "How do I let go and give him to God?"

It wasn't easy. Breathing was hard sometimes, and fear had a grip on my heart. But isn't courage doing things even when we're afraid? And so I continued holding the boundary until I saw patterns from my husband that moved toward the reestablishment of safety.

The righteous use of boundaries can be a powerful way we fight for the hearts of our husbands, and when we draw that line in the sand, we invite our husbands to battle for our hearts in return. Boundaries offer our loved ones the opportunity to choose higher, holier ground while providing protection for ourselves.

Surrendering whatever their choice is as we honor their agency can be incredibly frightening. It can be helpful to keep in mind the original revelation that we receive to set the boundary. Reminding ourselves that the boundary we set was inspired by God can help us to not loosen boundaries prematurely.

I hope we can all hold ourselves in compassion as we try to do hard things in new ways. It's okay if learning to implement boundaries is a process. Maybe we don't do as well as we would have liked in the beginning. That's okay. We can evaluate and try again another day.

I imagine many righteous women dressed in the full armor of God as we fight in new ways for our husbands and families. As daughters of God, we should not accept destructive patterns that might lead to the devastation of our homes. We are fighting an invisible war, and righteous boundaries are a part of divine strategy.

I stand resolutely by the statement that boundaries are brave, and you are brave to consider them.

> *What do you think about the concept of boundaries being courageous?*

Boundaries from the Garden

The first recorded boundary is also an amazing template.

"And I, the Lord God, commanded the man, saying: Of every tree of the garden thou mayest freely eat, but of the tree of the knowledge of good and evil, thou shalt not eat of it, nevertheless, thou mayest choose for thyself, for it is given unto thee; but, remember that I forbid it, for in the day thou eatest thereof thou shalt surely die" (Moses 3: 16–17).

In essence, Heavenly Father is saying, "I want to bless you with 'every tree that is pleasant to the sight and good for food' (Abraham 5:9). You can eat as much of these fruits as you would like, and I want you to enjoy them! But there's this *one* tree that I don't want you to eat from. In fact, I'm going to command you to not eat the fruit from that tree. You get to decide if you will choose to follow this boundary or not. If you choose to eat the fruit from the tree that I have forbidden, there will be a consequence, and here's what it is."

The more that I've pulled this template apart, the more I've learned. It is straightforward and gentle *and* it honors agency. It offers something that Heavenly Father wants to give us, followed by a commandment, followed by the option to choose, and finally followed by a consequence if it is broken.

Here's how this formula can be worded to form a boundary:

1. You are important to me, and I love you. I want to be close to you and spend time with you.
2. In order to be close to you, I need _____. (A few examples might be for him to not look at pornography, treat me kindly, or show humility.)
3. You can choose whether or not you will provide this need.

4. If you choose to not honor this request, then I will _____. (Some ideas might be requesting physical space, going out with a friend instead of going on a date, or practicing soul-care.)

I will share some examples of using this template, with the understanding that consequences should be discussed with God. The consequences that I share should not be taken as your specific answer:

- Example 1: I would like to snuggle you on the couch, and in order for me to do that, I need you to repair what you just said. If you aren't in a good emotional place to do that right now, I will go to the other room. I will also need physical space until repair is made.
- Example 2: I want to go out to dinner with you, but it hurts when we are together and you stare at other women. I won't force you to not stare at other women. However, if you stare at women when we are at the restaurant, I will call a friend or an Uber to pick me up.
- Example 3: I want to be close to you and build a wonderful life together. However, compulsive pornography use is causing chaos in our home and is affecting many things, including my own emotional stability. I can't make you see a qualified therapist. However, until you do, I need to have my own space in our room and request that you sleep in another area of the house.

Moroni gives a wonderful example of using this formula when defending his people against Zerahemnah. Here's the issue: the Nephites needed safety from the Lamanites who were trying to kill them, their rights of worship were being threatened, and their homes and lands were in jeopardy. By the grace of God, the Nephites were able to surround the Lamanites, and at this point, Moroni set a boundary similar to the example from the Garden of Eden. It looked something like this (see Alma 43–44):

1. We do not wish to fight you, and we want to offer you the opportunity to go home to your families.
2. In order for us to stop the fighting, we need you to surrender your weapons and make a covenant of peace.
3. You can choose if you will do this or not.
4. If you do not surrender your weapons of war and make a covenant of peace, we will continue to fight.

The Savior also used boundaries. To one man, the Savior said, "Sin no more, lest a worse thing come unto thee" (John 5:14). To the woman taken in adultery, He was gentle and kind and also added this boundary: "Go and sin no more" (John 8:11).

Remember when Jesus turned the tables in the temple? This was Him following through on a boundary to not treat the temple in disrespectful ways. We can see He was thoughtful about this event because John 2:15 says that "when he had made a scourge of small cords, he drove them all out of the temple." Basically, He took the time to think through what He would do in enough detail that he handmade the whip.

And yes, Christ did say to turn the other cheek. But I believe this counsel can be misunderstood and go beyond the mark. Compulsive behaviors and abusive behaviors are patterns. He did not say to turn the other cheek, then turn the other cheek again, and so on. We only have two cheeks. (Though my fun "cheeky" friend likes to remind me that we actually have four cheeks.)

Destructive patterns require interruption or else they can decimate individuals and families.

Is there a destructive pattern in your relationship with your loved one that needs to be interrupted? If so, explain.

Assignment should you choose:
Practice wording a boundary using the four-step guideline. Use your own words to write the following:

Step 1: I want to offer _____. (For example, closeness, relationship privileges, presence, etc.)

Step 2: In order to be close to you, I need _____. (A few examples might be for him to not look at pornography, treat you kindly, or show humility.)

Step 3: You can choose whether or not you will provide this need. (Word this in your own way.)

Step 4: If you choose to not honor this request, then I will _____. (Some ideas might be requesting physical space, going out with a friend instead of going on a date, or practicing soul-care.)

Observing as Part of a Boundary

Sometimes it is simply our role to observe what our spouse is and isn't doing from a detached perspective. Such periods can be difficult, and it can feel like we aren't accomplishing much. However, more is typically happening than we can sometimes see.

During the Creation of the earth, the "Gods watched those things which they had ordered until they obeyed" (Abraham 4:18). Elements do things differently when they are being observed, and oftentimes, so do people.

Consider how the following observation might sound like an accomplishment plus a challenge to continue improving as a spouse: "I appreciate that you looked away when you seemed triggered regarding that attractive woman in the store. It's normal to notice someone's beauty, and I appreciate that you were aware of your personal limits. It helped me to feel safer with you at that moment. I look forward to more moments of safety."

The observation in this example acknowledges positive action, a lessening of shame, an awareness that they are being observed to some extent, and a challenge to keep up the good work. It also offers an opportunity to connect in similar ways in the future.

None of this means we need to look over our spouse's shoulder all the time, nor should we consider ourselves to be their guardian. Honoring agency is critical. Also, when they realize they are being observed by us when we are grounded and detached, it can sometimes encourage them to improve. Should they choose not to improve or fall short at times, we can create and implement the needed boundaries.

What about Covenants?

New concepts can be like horse pills: hard to swallow. At least that was my experience a few years ago before my change of heart regarding boundaries. I was having a phone conversation with my dear friend Katy Willis, and I was not shy about sharing that I did not think boundaries were a righteous principle. Katy held her ground as she gently pushed back. She saw that I felt trapped in an unfaithful and sometimes emotionally abusive marriage. In my mind, because I had made covenants, I was expected to protect those covenants at all costs. This line of thinking was fertile ground for allowing myself to be treated poorly in an effort to keep those covenants intact. In truth, I wasn't protecting myself, my children, or my covenants well at that time.

"I've made covenants and I take them seriously," I argued. Katy reminded me that while I had kept my covenants, my husband had not. She explained that my covenants with God were secure. My husband could choose to repair his covenants, but that would need to be his choice and was not something I could do for him.

Katy later told me that during that phone conversation, she was sitting in the temple parking lot and was looking at the physical boundary of the fence protecting that sacred building. I find it a tender mercy that Heavenly Father allowed her to see that boundary at a time when I was challenging the concepts she was sharing.

As women who are striving to live *in* the world but not *of* the world, we often rely heavily on our covenants. We take them seriously and often do all we can to honor them. While this can be a noble attribute, we can go too far by enduring destructive patterns.

It's a good thing to hold our covenants sacred—*of course* we do all we can with God to heal our situations when He guides us to do so, especially when we have made covenants of an eternal nature. But it is also crucial to remember that we cannot make choices for our loved ones. They need to have the opportunity to choose whether or not they will keep their covenants to us and to Heavenly Father.

> *Holding yourself in compassion, consider if keeping covenants has seemed like a stumbling block for you in regard to setting boundaries. If so, how has that manifested in your responses or lack of responses?*

Marriage Covenants Depend on Three Beings

A marriage covenant includes both spouses and God and can be portrayed like this:

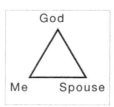

We have the power to keep our covenants, and God will always keep His covenants with us. However, we cannot control what our spouse does. When one party breaks their covenants, it might look more like this:

The hopeful thing about this illustration is that when a spouse breaks their covenants, our covenants with God are still intact. Also hopeful is that broken covenants can be repaired through the Atonement of Jesus Christ should our spouse be willing to participate in that process.

Having Heavenly Father as the third member in our covenant marriages means that what He says matters. He is personally involved and should be included in any decisions regarding staying or leaving marriages where covenants have been broken.

> How does understanding covenant relationships impact your decision-making process?

Covenants Are Not "Jailers"

I am not an advocate for or against divorce as a boundary in anyone's individual situation. No therapist, clergy, mentor, coach, family member, or friend can or should make that decision for anyone else. While feedback regarding staying or leaving can be immeasurably beneficial, the final decision should be made between the individual person and God.

Keeping in mind that my situation is severe, I'll share that when I didn't feel like divorce was an option, I felt hopeless. I felt trapped and like I could not make boundaries because my husband might leave, which would mean I would be without a covenant marriage, which would affect our children and me negatively throughout the eternities. There is a great deal of fear in this type of thinking. Ironically, these faulty understandings led to trying to control my husband and the situation, which did not honor his agency. I can offer myself a great deal of self-compassion regarding my actions during that period because I really didn't have the awareness or education to do much better at the time. When I learned more, I chose to do better.

I am thankful to see more clearly now, but regarding the consideration of divorce in severe situations, I want to share the following counsel from church leaders.

Elder Jeffrey R. Holland said, "It is . . . important for some of you living in real anguish to note what [the Savior] did *not* say. He did *not* say, 'You are not allowed to feel true pain or real sorrow from the shattering experiences you have had at the hand of another.' *Nor* did He say, 'In order to forgive fully, you have to reenter a toxic relationship or return to an abusive, destructive circumstance.'"[32]

Also, Elder Dallin H. Oaks said, "We know that many of you are innocent victims—members whose former spouses persistently betrayed sacred covenants or abandoned or refused to perform marriage responsibilities for an extended period. Members who have experienced such abuse have firsthand knowledge of circumstances worse than divorce. When a marriage is dead and beyond hope of resuscitation, it is needful to have a means to end it."[33]

Finally, President Nelson said, "If you are married to a companion who has broken his or her covenants, your willingness to let God prevail in your life will allow your covenants with God to remain intact. The Savior will heal your broken heart. The heavens will open as you seek to know how to move forward. You do not need to wander or wonder."[34]

Covenants should absolutely be taken seriously. Also, though, when we experience things like patterns of abuse, adultery (including compulsive pornography use), addiction, or abandonment in our covenant relationships, covenants can be mistakenly perceived as a sort of jailer. I do not believe this is what a loving Heavenly Father intends.

---

32. Jeffrey R. Holland, "The Ministry of Reconciliation," *Ensign* or *Liahona*, Nov. 2018, 79.
33. Dallin H. Oaks, "Divorce," *Ensign* or *Liahona*, May 2007, 70–71.
34. Russell M. Nelson, "Let God Prevail," *Ensign* or *Liahona*, Nov. 2020, 94.

Humble, Honest, Accountable, and Willing to Connect

In regard to boundaries, I have found humility, honesty, accountability, and a willingness to connect to be some of the best measuring sticks available. I learned about their importance as I have participated in the S.A. Lifeline Foundation, for which I am immensely grateful. They are foundational to the boundaries I set.

Several years ago, my husband had a stretch of two and a half years of sobriety, but he did not yet have the tools to be in recovery. It was a very rough time because he exhibited the attitudes and behaviors of addiction, even though he wasn't acting out. He white-knuckled his way through, would yell a lot, was not emotionally regulated, and more. I didn't see any acting-out behaviors during that period, so I didn't feel justified in setting boundaries. I would love to go back in time and take my younger self by the hand while I explain that I could indeed set boundaries based on humility, honesty, accountability, and a willingness to connect.

Because acting-out behaviors are often kept in the dark, it's easier for me to evaluate emotional safety by observing how the other person is implementing humility, honesty, accountability, and a willingness to connect.

Let's see how we can apply these principles to a couple of scenarios.

Made-up scenario 1: While searching for a bill in my husband's email account, I come across some opened emails that have explicit titles. I let my husband know what I found, and he becomes defensive. He tells me that someone else must have opened them and that he doesn't know where the emails came from. He then becomes angry that I was in his email account.

In this scenario, humility, honesty, accountability, and a willingness to connect are all missing. He is not humble or willing to connect when he's defensive, and he's not being honest or accountable about opening the emails. He is also not showing accountability, humility, or a willingness to connect when he does not acknowledge the pain that I am in due to his behaviors.

Made-up scenario 2: My husband asks if he can talk to me about a slip. During our conversation, he is honest about having lustful thoughts that turned into fantasizing about women. He is aware that his behavior hurts me, and he genuinely apologizes without justifying his behavior. He talks to me about ways he can have better internal and external boundaries for himself in the future, and he makes an action plan with his sponsor. He then gives me the physical and emotional space I might need or request, or he gives me the comfort I might need should that be my desire.

The power in placing a boundary on humility, honesty, accountability, and a willingness to connect is that we don't usually need proof of acting-out behaviors to implement said boundary. When we place a boundary around the root behaviors, we are less likely to get caught up in the details that can more easily be manipulated or argued about. Acting-out behaviors create chaos. Looking past the chaos and into root issues provides clarity, decreases the need to find hidden details, and is empowering.

> *Consider an interaction with your spouse that was painful. Can you point out where humility, honesty, accountability, or a willingness to connect might have been missing?*

Thoughts on Boundaries and Humility

Humility deserves some individual tender loving care because it is easy to misunderstand. When looking for genuine humility, it's important to note that humility is neither puffing up nor shrinking. Puffing up can be easier to spot. Shrinking, such as when our loved ones say self-degrading things, is not humility.

For instance, instead of saying something humble such as "I am truly sorry that I betrayed your trust, and it makes sense that you are hurting," they might instead say "I'm such a failure for doing that!" or "I can't do anything right." When shameful attitudes are adopted, instead of attending to you and the pain that has been caused, they want to be reassured that they aren't bad. This puts the focus on themselves instead of on the person who was harmed.

Someone who is showing true humility will own the truth and acknowledge the pain they have caused without the focus being on them. This often takes practice and healing.

> *Evaluate how your loved one has shown humility or how humility might need to improve in order for you to feel connected in healthy ways in your relationship.*

Placing Boundaries on Disconnect

One of those scriptures that can stab me right in the heart when there is disconnect in my marriage is Abraham 5:14: "It is not good for man [or woman] to be alone." In order to act out in sexual compulsions and addictions, there must be isolation of some sort, which causes a disconnect in a marriage relationship. Disconnection can be emotionally, physically, and spiritually painful. Pain is normal under these circumstances and can even be helpful to notice because it is by divine design that we long for connection in a covenant relationship.

A common pattern of behavior when someone is engaged in compulsions or addictions is to disconnect from those who are closest to them. Disconnecting is often part of the acting-out process and is therefore a good and often necessary thing to place a boundary on.

For instance, a boundary around disconnect that I have is that I need to feel emotionally connected with my husband before engaging in physical intimacy.

Also, if I have tried to connect with my husband emotionally, and he pulls away for reasons he doesn't share, that's a red flag. I might protect myself with physical and emotional space from him until he chooses to own his behavior and choose connection.

One example of this might be that perhaps a spouse is choosing to stay later and later at work, which might create unsafe situations. A boundary might be necessary for such a scenario.

I'll share my personal process that may or may not be helpful to hear.

If, after trying to connect with my husband emotionally, there is still a disconnect on his end, I might take that to prayer. If I receive a spiritual confirmation that it's a good idea to put a boundary up regarding the disconnection, my boundary might sound something like this: "I have been hopeful that we can connect, but that does not seem to be reciprocated right now. You can choose whether to repair the connection or not. Until the connection is repaired, I need to have some physical and emotional space."

The next part is of great importance: I then need to take care of myself very, very well. Disconnection can be incredibly painful, and it's okay to protect myself from such patterns and to then replenish. Ample soul-care when the pain of disconnection is present is not frivolous. Soul-care is a way to function better in situations that might otherwise cripple us.

Such a boundary might hurt my husband, but his disconnection hurts me as well and is often part of the acting-out process.

I don't use the word *deserve* often, but I will here: I deserve to feel safe in my own home and in my marriage. Feeling safe is a need and not a petty desire. You deserve that as well, dear sister.

> Is your loved one showing a willingness to provide a kind, loving, and safe connection with you?

When to Lift Boundaries: Fixed versus Fluid

Learning to set boundaries is hard work, and thinking through what makes us feel unsafe and what we might need to feel safe again are both foundational.

In the beginning of recovery, it can be helpful to set well-defined boundaries. For example, "If you lie to me, I will need you to sleep separately for three days." There is a defined end to a boundary when this method is used.

Eventually, boundaries can evolve into being more fluid. This can look like the following: "When I feel safe again, I am willing to be physically and emotionally closer to you." There are specific reasons why there is no set time for a boundary that is fluid. For instance, if I do see patterns of behavior that suggest that humility, honesty, accountability, and a willingness to connect are present, the boundary might last shorter than a defined amount of time. Also, if I don't see patterns of change, I have not boxed myself into welcoming him back into my space before I am ready.

A word of caution to myself and anyone else who might need to hear this: the goal is to look for patterns of changed behavior and not a one-time event before completely lifting boundaries. It is easy to become overly excited when we see our loved ones do something good and to let down boundaries before trust has been earned.

When thinking of this concept, I like to remember Joseph of Egypt when he tests his brothers before restoring their relationship. To me, it seems like he wanted to know their hearts before deciding what boundaries to have and what boundaries to let go of. He was, in essence, trying to see if they had gained humility, honesty, accountability, and a willingness to connect. Joseph went to great efforts to evaluate his own safety with his brothers by observing whether or not they had changed, which included framing Benjamin for theft. It wasn't until Joseph could see that his brothers had truly changed that he let them know who he was and opened the door for relationships with them (see Genesis 42–45).

I am not suggesting that we test our spouses in such ways. However, it is important to have an attitude of "Good job on that—now let's wait and see if the pattern continues."

> Do you need to set a boundary? If so, would it be better in your situation if that boundary were fixed or fluid?

Internal Boundaries Regarding Being a Detective

My breath was shallow, my pulse was quickened, and I felt the adrenaline pumping through my body. The distress over what I might find . . . again . . . on my husband's computer was nearly crippling. I was short-tempered and anxious, and every muscle in my body was tight. I had searched and searched his computer for evidence. The more that I meticulously inspected his history, the faster my heart raced. My search was out of fear because I wanted to know my reality.

I was seeking safety.

Can you relate to such searches? It is normal to want to know the truth and to seek it out. It is normal to feel fear over our loved one's patterns of behavior and what we can't see. Detective-like behaviors (or hypervigilant behaviors) are attempts at finding safety by striving to learn what the truth of our situation is.

Hypervigilance is a catch-22 of sorts and can keep us stuck in excruciating pain while increasing feelings of anxiety, sometimes to unmanageable levels.

Is looking for evidence of acting-out behaviors *always* a self-destructive act? That's a definite no in my book. I have had direct revelation that guided me to find information that I definitely needed, and I've heard many women share similar experiences. I believe that checking the history of a spouse who has a pattern of dishonesty is a partner's right, though this opinion is controversial.

Other times, though, I have searched for the truth out of fear.

Well-defined boundaries around safety checks can help us because the irony is that safety-seeking behaviors rarely leave one feeling safe.

My personal boundary when checking my husband's history is this: If I feel a prompting to check, it's okay to do so. If I don't feel a prompting and check anyway, that's a slip on my part. Also, though, if I do slip, I strive to offer myself ample self-compassion for wanting to know my reality. I also strive to make a plan for making different choices in the future.

If we don't know what our loved one has been doing because we haven't seen with our eyes or heard with our ears, we are not left without options. We can still protect ourselves with the guidance of the Holy Ghost, who can help us navigate when we physically cannot see.

Remember the law of the harvest from chapter 4? Very often when compulsions and addictions are sown, the fruit is a lack of humility, honesty, accountability, and willingness to connect. This is a prime example of why there is power in placing boundaries on those root issues. In some ways, it doesn't matter that we can't see proof with our eyes—the fruit of acting-out behaviors is often before us. This does not mean that when a lack of humility, honesty, accountability, and willingness to connect are present that we know that our loved one is acting out. However, it does mean that when we see that their behaviors are off in these areas, our safety is compromised and boundaries are likely a very good idea.

I'm sending you lots of compassion if you have experienced hypervigilance. I get it. You want to know your truth. Me too, sister. Me too.

Have you participated in safety-seeking, detective-like behaviors regarding your spouse? If so, how has that affected you?

Can you currently offer yourself self-compassion regarding detective-like or safety-seeking behaviors? If not, perhaps make a commitment to practice self-compassion.

What internal boundaries might you need in the future for detective-like behaviors?

Disconnecting with Love

Disconnecting with love is such a freeing concept. In essence, it honors our agency and that of our spouse while allowing us to live in greater peace.

It sounds so easy, but if you're anything like me, detaching with love can be a hard concept to grasp. Take heart though! It takes practice and intentional effort, but it can be understood and has the power to change lives.

Do you remember the rich young man who asked the Savior what he needed to do to enter into the kingdom of heaven? At first, he seemed relieved to hear Jesus name some commandments he was already following. However, when he asked, "What lack I yet?" the Savior gave him counsel that was specific to him: "Go and sell that thou hast, and give to the poor, and thou shalt have treasure in heaven: and come and follow me" (Matthew 19:21). You'll remember that the rich young man goes away sorrowing.

What is notable about this exchange is what the Savior did *not* do. The Savior did not chase the young man. He did not beg him to make a different choice, nor did He pout, nor did He say *anything* else. He lets the young man know the boundary that He specifically needs to meet and then *lets him choose* (see Matthew 19:16–26).

(Side note: I like to imagine and hope that the young man needed to process this request and that he later chose to follow the counsel from the Savior.)

Disconnecting with love requires a serenity that is built on the Savior. It requires us to have faith in a bigger plan than our own and the knowledge that no matter what our loved one chooses, we will be alright in the long run.

It can be painful to disconnect with love from someone we want to be close to. I have found that how I word my intentions matters. I still want to be my best self and do my part in calming situations.

I will share my basic process for disconnecting with love:

- Step 1: Internally recognize some errors in what is being said or done.
- Step 2: Find the emotion that the other person is experiencing and genuinely validate and connect with it.
- Step 3: Mention something short about how I see that differently—without begging, chasing, arguing, or explaining.
- Step 4: Disconnect from the situation.

For instance, while in active addiction, my husband can say things that I strongly disagree with. I have exerted great effort toward trying to talk him out of such thoughts, but those efforts have rarely fixed his thought processes. Most often, my efforts prove futile when he is in this mental state.

Using the steps mentioned above, I might start by recognizing the unhealthy thinking in my husband. Next, I gently say something like this: "It seems like you might be feeling distressed. I sometimes feel distressed as well and relate to that emotion. I see this situation differently, but I won't try to talk you out of what you are saying." And then I walk away and do something that will replenish my soul.

It feels different in my body when my husband and I disconnect with love because we do not argue, we honor agency, and both parties' dignity stays intact.

> With self-compassion, can you think of a recent incident where detaching with love might have helped? If so, how might you have handled the situation differently? (Note: the goal is not to shame ourselves but rather to evaluate so we can improve next time.)

9
Honoring Emotions

Feeling numb can be incredibly unsettling. Numbness has its place, such as calming us after a traumatic experience, but it's no place to live. And I was definitely living there.

I knew I needed to grieve some things regarding my husband's addiction, but I just couldn't. I had no tears.

I discussed this in therapy. I intentionally watched sad movies, reached out to friends, and listened to sad songs. Nothing. Still no tears.

Around this period of time, my husband was in active addiction, but I didn't know that. I did know he was treating me poorly, and I frequently poured my heart out in prayer to Heavenly Father over this subject.

One morning, I was praying on my bathroom floor about what I was experiencing. Heavenly Father's response took me by surprise: "I am angry with Bart."

I thought, "You're angry at my husband?" I didn't know that anger was allowed. And then I made a choice. If Heavenly Father could get angry with Bart, then so could I. And I *let* the anger come.

What happened next fascinated me: torrential sobs, red eyes, and a runny nose. I have never been so relieved to be a mess as I was at that time, and it was also reassuring to feel something again, even if it wasn't a cheerful emotion.

This experience helped me to learn that every emotion is important to honor.

Experiencing anger was also critical because it told me that what I was experiencing was not alright, and it helped me set some needed boundaries.

Interesting to me was the newfound understanding that emotions aren't good or bad—they just are. A full range of emotions provides a wide spectrum of experience, richness, and depth to life.

> Have you considered emotions to be good, bad, or something else? Explain.

THE SAVIOR AND EMOTIONS

The Savior is emotionally complex. He felt and expressed love as no other being has before or since. He weeps with people, even though He knows that He will soon dry their tears with a miracle. He was a "man of sorrows, acquainted with grief" (Isaiah 53:3). Jesus celebrated things like weddings, which typically involve feelings of joy. Have you looked up the word *anger* in the scriptures? Surprising to me was seeing that many of the scriptures on anger are regarding the *Lord* being angry.

Let's revisit some of the emotions that the Savior experienced, from the list found in chapter 2:

- Joy (see Hebrews 12:2)
- Sorrow (see Mark 14:34)
- Grief (see Isaiah 53:3)
- Anger (Because there are several scriptures about the Lord being angry, I have selected one from each major book of scripture as examples: see Psalm 85:3; John 2:13–17; 2 Nephi 19:17; Doctrine and Covenants 61:5; Moses 7:34)
- Delight (see Doctrine and Covenants 76:5)
- Compassion (see Romans 9:15)
- Empathy (see Moses 7:28; John 11:35–36)
- Agony (see Luke 22:44)
- Jealousy (see Exodus 20:5; Mosiah 11:22)

I wonder, What if learning to experience emotions is part of God's plan for us? Also, if Christ can feel all these emotions, why do I sometimes limit what I "should" and "should not" feel? Do you do that sometimes too? And what if experiencing a wide range of emotions allows me to feel more deeply and to relate with others better? Maybe experiencing emotions can help me become closer to the Savior.

Let's dig deeper.

> *Does it make a difference to you to know that the Savior experienced emotions? Why or why not?*

Hmm . . . That's Curious

It's an incredibly human thing to decide that we know something logically. Exploring why we are feeling something with curiosity is an act of faith, courage, and humility. Curiosity requires us to question our own logic, challenge our own conclusions, and consider things that don't fit into the narrative we have created. Curiosity is, at its center, a display of humility because it requires us to move out of the belief that we know most things.

It also uses a different part of the brain when we stay curious. Shifting the focus of a situation toward curiosity helps minimize shame, aids us in staying open to other possibilities, and can even help us shift out of a trauma state.

One example of using curiosity might be that I am feeling rejected. When I am not staying curious about why I am experiencing feelings of rejection, it's easy for me to come to false conclusions, such as "There must be something incredibly wrong with me." If, though, I am staying curious, I can better observe and wonder if maybe the other person is struggling with things that I cannot see or understand. Perhaps my perception was off. Or maybe there is something I can repair in that relationship. I might even be able to see that this is not something I can fix and that I actually need a boundary. Or something else.

It can also be helpful to be curious about why other people behave as they do. For instance, there are common misunderstandings about those who struggle with sexual compulsions and addictions. It can be easy to judge someone incorrectly for such behaviors. Curiosity allows us to consider factors other than behavior alone as to why someone has acted out in such ways. A few common factors I have noticed in those who struggle with compulsions or addictions include that they have often experienced abandonment of some kind, various forms of abuse, and early exposure to pornography, among other childhood factors. There are also possibilities that those who struggle with compulsions or addictions might have neurodivergent traits, mental illness, personality disorders, major life changes, and more.

Staying curious about behavior and beliefs helps us to explore root causes. When the Savior heals the root, better results occur. Curiosity is critical because we don't usually take things so personally when we wonder versus when we think we know.

One of my favorite places to be curious is on my knees. Like the prophet Nephi once asked, "Have ye inquired of the Lord?" (1 Nephi 15:8). When I am curious with Heavenly Father, I gain the opportunity to practice learning how He communicates with me. I don't always hear clear answers, and He doesn't always answer me in those moments. But still, I learn when I practice.

Leaning into Emotions

"I like to sit in uncomfortable emotions," said no one ever. It can be distressing and painful, and it's an intensely vulnerable thing to do. Learning to honor painful emotions can also be an important thing to practice.

I once had the opportunity to interview someone about this subject, and here's what I learned: Do you know the difference between buffaloes and cows in a storm? Cows see a storm coming and run away from the storm, but buffaloes see the storm coming and charge into it. The cow's time in the storm is prolonged, while the buffalo's time in the storm is shortened.[35]

That's like emotions as well. Leaning into emotions helps us experience them and move through them. This is a skill that can be learned, and it can be incredibly beneficial.

After one intense period of grieving, I was surprised to feel gratitude from the Savior. I have reflected on why that is and have come to see that willingly experiencing some of the pain that comes from being human allows me a little more insight into what the Savior experienced. It is easy to misunderstand and to minimize what I and others are going through if I don't know some heartache and pain. Christ doesn't trivialize our pain, and though He *can* instantly take it away, oftentimes He instead chooses to stay

---

35. See Ashlynn Mitchell and Jeni Brockbank, "Ep. 21 Be the Buffalo With Ashlynn Mitchell," July 27, 2021, in *Betrayal Trauma SOS*, podcast.

by our side as we experience it. His example in doing this is the essence of "mourn[ing] with those who mourn and . . . comfort[ing] those who stand in need of comfort" (Mosiah 18:9).

Another benefit is that at some point, the Savior inevitably lifts us out of the heartache and dries our tears. Experiencing this divine comfort can help us learn about the Savior and what He can do through the Atonement. Such experiences can deepen our relationship with Him. The relieving promise is that "the Lord God will wipe away tears from off all faces" (Isaiah 25:8). "All faces" surely includes yours and mine.

The Savior has a beautiful ability to "succor" His people. Elder Holland said this: "[*Succor*] is used often in the scriptures to describe Christ's care for and attention to us. It means literally 'to run to.' What a magnificent way to describe the Savior's urgent effort on our behalf. Even as he calls us to come to him and follow him, he is unfailingly running to help us"[36] It makes my soul sigh realizing that He has, He can, and He will run to me in my times of distress. The same is true for you as well.

When this has happened in my own situation, the power of the Atonement is made real in melt-worthy ways. I gain a better relationship with the Savior, and my eyes become open in new ways that allow me to connect with others and minister more effectively. The timing for this relief is always offered on His timeline and rarely happens as quickly as I would like.

> Is there an emotion you might like to intentionally honor while leaning into the Savior? If so, what is it?

Getting Stuck in Emotions and Learning to Shift

I was kind of dreading group therapy one particular week. For several weeks, there had been a heaviness in the air that lingered, and I brought that heaviness home with me. Thankfully, our therapist noticed as well and suggested that we intentionally shift into some happiness. That day, we took

---

36. Jeffrey R. Holland, "Come unto Me" (Brigham Young University devotional, Mar. 2, 1997), 9, speeches.byu.edu.

a break from heartache as each person shared something that had recently brought us joy.

What a relief that break was, and I learned a lesson that has remained with me: emotions are something to honor and experience, but getting stuck in any emotion for a long period of time is not helpful.

For instance, I once "managed" my emotions by rejecting emotional pain and trying to be happy all the time. This led to me not recognizing dangerous and destructive patterns. Positive outlooks are wonderful as long as they are based in truth.

An example of this is anger. Anger can be an amazing motivator to create change. (Take, for example, the Savior as He cleansed the temple). But also consider that one can get stuck in anger, or it can get out of control, which can lead to devastating destruction. Anger is sort of like a fire: it can roast your marshmallow or burn down the forest. Interesting to me is that often when the Lord is angry, He almost always does something about it. There's typically an action, or a boundary, associated with His anger. Sometimes the Lord kindles His anger as an action and sometimes there is another consequence. (For examples, see Exodus 4:14; Hebrews 3: 8–11; Ether 14:25; Doctrine and Covenants 63:1.) Learning that anger sometimes has a divine purpose and when and how to appropriately act on it can be helpful in shifting out of anger.

Sadness is important to feel at times as well. However, living in sadness for long periods of time and without reprieve can lead to other things like depression.

Consider when someone uses humor in wonderful ways to lighten moods and find joyful connection. But humor can also be turned into great pain and a lack of connection when the comedian can't shift into needed conversations with an appropriate level of seriousness.

As a spouse of someone who displays patterns of sexual betrayal, you may find yourself becoming overwhelmed by many different emotions. Thus, learning to shift is an important component to a good recovery.

> *Are you experiencing a "stuck" emotion? If so, explain. Consider what might help you shift away from it.*

Additional Tools for Shifting

As we move into learning about grief and mourning, the power of shifting can be critical so that no emotion will overtake us.

Here are a few tools to consider when intentionally shifting:

- Give grief a designated place. For instance, maybe give yourself a period of time every day (like twenty to thirty minutes) to cry if you need to. This can be relieving to have the time set aside to mourn and can help you know that tomorrow you get the same time to grieve if you need it. This exercise allows there to be an end to the pain, even if it's temporary.
- Do something opposite of the emotion you are stuck in. For instance, if you feel trapped in sadness, maybe put on a happy song and dance to it.
- Perhaps find clean comedy sketches to watch, which allow you to intentionally seek out joy and laughter in the midst of pain. It's amazing what fifteen minutes of laughter can do for a soul.
- If physical movement is difficult because of emotional pain, it can be helpful to consider some gentle body movement.
- Do something creative. Creating not only engages the frontal cortex in the brain, but it also engages our spirits. President Dieter F. Uchtdorf said, "We each have an inherent wish to create something that did not exist before. . . . Creation brings deep satisfaction and fulfillment. We develop ourselves and others when we take unorganized matter into our hands and mold it into something of beauty."[37]
- Sometimes when I am anxious, I will do a brain dump. I might set a one- to three-minute timer and write down all the things that are bothering me. I often feel a relief from burdens after doing this.
- Surrender is a powerful tool to help us shift into peace. I love how surrender is taught in S.A. Lifeline: "knees, phone, box." After writing down what we would like to surrender, we first pray about it (knees). Then we speak it out loud to someone else (phone). And

---

37. Dieter F. Uchtdorf, "Happiness, Your Heritage," *Ensign* or *Liahona*, Nov. 2008, 118.

finally, we place our written surrender somewhere (box). This might be a box or the trash can, or you might even burn it.

Any of these activities can be viewed as intentional soul-care. Each activity requires self-awareness of what emotion we are trapped in and a certain amount of brainstorming to determine what might help us shift.

> *Are you needing to shift from an emotion right now? If so, is there an activity that might sound good for you to try?*
>
> <u>Assignment should you choose:</u>
> *Create or buy a surrender box or container. Some people might like to have a picture of the Savior on their surrender box or other meaningful things like scriptures. When you are distressed, participate in the surrender process described above: "knees, phone, box."*

The Power of Grief

Tears are sacred. God counts them. Sometimes He even weeps with us.

The pain of grief is the frequent birthplace for awe-inspiring awareness, new depths of compassion within ourselves, and a relationship with the Savior that can feel melt-worthy.

I once rejected the notion of grieving most anything except for death, but then I had a personal experience that deeply impacted me.

As part of the group therapy program I attended, I created a "Losses Poster." The assignment included drawing out the losses I had experienced as the spouse of someone with a sexual addiction. I then presented my chicken-scratch "artwork" to my fellow group members.

For lost time due to addiction, I sketched a clock. Losses in finances because of acting-out behaviors were represented with a messily drawn dollar bill. My concern for my eternal marriage covenant was symbolized with a simply drawn temple, and so on.

I then presented my poster to my group, who beautifully validated what I had been through and related in their own ways. I felt seen and heard as they truly mourned with and comforted me. Also, my eyes were opened to the severity of my situation, and scales of denial began to fall away.

I was unprepared for the bombardment of grief that followed.

It's notable that my previous attempts at feeling better from hard things mostly involved staying busy. Pushing the pain down was my norm and is likely why I had nearly twenty years of heartache to mourn. My therapist had recommended leaning into the grief, and though I was hesitant, I decided to try it on for size this time.

This new experiment took my breath away as I was overcome by a tsunami of emotion that followed, and I was mostly a lump on my couch for the following two weeks. I treated myself gently, and I didn't push away the pain this time. It felt unbearable at times, but much to my amazement, I was not alone. The Savior held my hand and stayed by my side.

Something that surprised me was when it felt like the Savior was grateful that I was willing to face pain in this way. The Savior was *grateful* that I was willing to endure pain? And yet it was clear to me that He was indeed grateful. I think He knows how intensely this experience changed me and that I will be a more effective child of God because I experienced sorrow and redemption.

I remember the day that it felt as if the Savior took me by the hand and lifted me out of the intense grief. I was relieved. I felt changed at a soul-deep level. I felt closer to my Savior, and I now count it as one of the most sacred experiences of my life.

I came to better understand Matthew 5:4: "Blessed are they that mourn; for they shall be comforted."

Assignment should you choose:
Consider honoring the losses you have experienced from your loved one's patterns of betrayal. Here are a few ideas to do this:

Draw symbols to represent your losses on a poster and discuss your poster with someone safe.

List your losses due to your loved one's behavior and share that with someone safe.

Honoring Grief: A (Surprisingly) Christlike Practice

"Do you think the Savior was changed by the Atonement?" my dad asked me a few years ago. It was a beautiful question that has rung in my heart ever since.

At the root of the Atonement seems to be an unfathomable amount of grief and mourning. Isaiah 53:3 tells us that He was a "man of sorrows, acquainted with grief."

I'm struck with reverential wonderment as I consider the Savior being willing to delve deep into my own mists of darkness. Talk about empathy on a whole new level.

I don't know how the Savior could have not been changed by the Atonement. Knowing our griefs and sorrows gives Him incredible insight into who we are and why we do the things we do.

Consider with me our baptismal covenant to "mourn with those who mourn and to comfort those who stand in need of comfort" (Mosiah 18:9).

I am not usually qualified to comfort others until I have paid the price to relate on some level with why and how they would need to be comforted. I am not the Savior and do not have the capacity to understand each individual heartache and pain. I can, however, search deep and mourn with the Savior regarding my own trials. When I do this, I inevitably emerge with an expansion to better understand and minister in new and deeper ways.

A few ways I have been changed by mourning include being much less judgmental, being better able to sit with others in pain without trying to fix them, and being able to more genuinely offer my own experience, faith, and hope while letting others walk their own path with the Savior.

The rewards I have experienced in regard to how I see and respond to myself are things I consider to be of eternal value as well. Because of mourning, I have better accepted my circumstances and can make wiser choices for addressing them. I have a great deal more self-compassion, and I can more easily accept love, compassion, and service from others.

Mourning can change us in ways that are fundamental to our eternal growth, and as we mourn, we gain a better awareness of how to better serve others. Much like putting a bandage over skin that has a splinter in it without first extracting the splinter, skipping mourning can prolong undercurrents of pain that can seem to plague us.

I relate to the notion that it can be difficult to willingly enter into the pain that mourning creates. It is helpful for me to remember that intense mourning has a shelf life.

The Savior is qualified to lift us out of those states, and He has and will do just that in His own way, which often includes the assistance of others. For instance, some might need to mourn under the supervision of a qualified professional, while others might need the help of medication.

I am sending you great love as you find your custom, tailor-made way of mourning with the Savior. Grief is an incredibly brave and vulnerable thing to willingly participate in.

> *Consider what's taught in Matthew 5:4: "Blessed are they that mourn; for they shall be comforted." How might this scripture apply to you and your situation with your loved one?*

Grieving Living Circumstances

Why would someone need to grieve a living person or situation? In a nutshell, grief helps us find truth and live in it with our eyes wide open. And yes, that can be an excruciating process.

For me, experiencing grief was an important aspect of letting go of control to better understand the severity of my situation, and it allowed me to create better boundaries.

When someone has a serious physical illness or experiences the death of a loved one, it's easy to offer them grace, empathy, and even material things such as meals. But when there is a need to grieve living loved ones and situations, the support is not as readily recognized or offered, even though those who suffer certainly need it.

Finding support to grieve living circumstances is sometimes necessary and even imperative. While it can be challenging to find those who are able to mourn something or someone who is still living, it is possible. If I could go back in time, I would tell my pre-recovery self, "Find your people, Jeni! They will walk with you through this heartache."

I want to offer my own empathy to those who are needing to mourn living circumstances. I know that grieving living circumstances is a terribly painful experience and can also be isolating, which is most regrettable. I offer my experience, faith, and hope that it is beneficial to seek out those who have been qualified through their own fiery furnace, and it's especially helpful to heavily lean on the Savior. I send much love and prayer to those who are suffering in such ways.

> Do you have a living circumstance to grieve with Christ? If so, what is it?

10

A Commitment to the Truth

Regarding this chapter, please note that when I started working to face the truth of my entire situation, it took my breath away. I needed the support of a qualified professional and a community of women who understood. I also needed a period of time to grieve in order to see and accept the truth.

This was my experience, and yours might be different. In any case, please heal in wisdom and order. Consider the support you need to find necessary healing.

Different Parts of an Elephant

If you were blind, how might you describe an elephant if you only felt the leg? Or what if you felt just the tail, only the trunk, or just an ear?

President Uchtdorf talked about a poem about six men who were blind and who felt different parts of an elephant. He summarized their individual conclusions: "One of the men finds the elephant's leg and describes it as being round and rough like a tree. Another feels the tusk and describes the elephant as a spear. A third grabs the tail and insists that an elephant is like a rope. A fourth discovers the trunk and insists that the elephant is like a large snake."[38]

---

38. Dieter F. Uchtdorf, "What Is Truth?" (Brigham Young University devotional, Jan. 13, 2013), 1, speeches.byu.edu.

Sometimes we genuinely don't know what the secret behaviors of our spouses are. Other times, though, we have self-protective blinders on that prevent us from seeing the whole truth about our situations.

For instance, because my husband faithfully opened my door for me, I would focus on him being a gentleman. I would tell others about this service he did for me and often reminded myself of his good qualities. However, after the door closed, he often did not display very gentlemanly behaviors or speech. I was so intent on seeing the good that I missed the entirety of my situation, which was severe.

If my marriage was an elephant, I might have been describing the ear, but in the process, I missed the entire body, trunk, and many other important elements. The thing is, the ear is an important part of an elephant. We do want to see the good, but we also want to live in truth.

Have you zoomed out to look at a larger picture of your situation? What does the whole of your situation look like? Are you, like me, only describing part of an entire elephant?

> *If you were to describe the behavior of your loved one as a whole, including good traits and also behaviors that need to be improved, what would that whole view look like?*

Committing to the Truth about Me

Can you imagine going to the ER with a very real problem, but when the receptionist at the check-in desk asks how they can help you, you reply, "Oh, I'm doing fine, thank you," then with a pasted smile on your face, you walk away?

With theatrical prowess, I have performed such shenanigans in regard to emotional pain. I am well equipped to let everyone, including myself, know that I am "fine."

Only . . . what if I'm *not* fine?

I think I walked around on an emotional "broken leg" of sorts for many years. Sure, it hurt terribly, and yes, it even got worse, but I just pushed that pain *way* down deep and kept going. My motto was something like "I am strong! Emotions are weak! I avoid pain like it's a plague!" Repeat.

The thing is, though, my way hadn't worked. I was hurting. I felt lonely. I needed more tools for healing and didn't have them. Finally admitting to myself that I couldn't heal on my own was the beginning of my own recovery.

It's easy to live in denial, and most everyone does it to some extent. Peeling away denial is sort of like peeling back layers of an onion, and it is a brave thing to do because it typically requires a commitment to truth, honoring grief, and a lot of humility.

Oh yeah, and stripping away denial can sometimes hurt too. A lot.

There are a few things I have had denial about and sometimes still chip away at. For example, I might think that my husband's acting-out behavior wasn't "that bad." I also minimized responsibility for my own actions and reactions, and I didn't see that I needed my own recovery.

Choosing to shed denial has some costs associated with it. For instance, denial can feel like a warm blanket, and when it's ripped away it can feel like that cuddly security is missing. We can feel exposed, embarrassed, emotionally naked, overcome with grief, and more. In short, ouch, ouch, ouch.

However, after the wound heals, we have more information to make better choices. We can get the help we need, find out we are not alone, and make decisions based on education, wisdom, and guidance from the Spirit. Facing the entirety about ourselves can help us find the calm that accompanies acceptance.

It is brave to lean into living in truth, and it is necessary in order to find deep healing. If we don't tell ourselves and the doctor that we have an infection, then the doctor can't prescribe the needed medication.

> *Are you hurting more than you admit? If so, what does that look like?*
>
> *Being very honest with yourself, answer this: how are you doing?*

COMMITTING TO THE TRUTH ABOUT MY SITUATION

My husband and I have gone on weekly dates religiously for most of our marriage. Even when things were hard, we would plan to go out, set up rules about not talking about hard things, and escape for a couple of hours. Even still, his behavior—especially if he was engaging in active addiction—could spill out on our dates.

I remember telling my friend about an incident on a date where my husband treated me poorly. My friend and I walked in silence for a while when she finally stopped, looked me in the eyes, and said, "I'm just wondering why you date him."

I thought, "Well, it seems like Church leaders say to go on frequent dates, and my parents dated each other weekly, and that seemed to work out for them. That's the formula. You date your spouse, and you end up happily ever after."

The only problem was that I *had* gone on dates with my husband faithfully for nearly two decades by that point, and I was definitely *not* living my "happily ever after."

I realized I had missed something obvious and came to learn that when I dated my husband during times when he was treating me poorly, my husband felt justified in his behavior. He thought he was doing better as a husband and father than he actually was.

Shifting my thinking took humility and work. The rewards, though, paid off in amazing ways. Here's a synopsis.

I started to set the boundary that I would like to date my husband but could not if he treated me poorly before or during the date. As I set this boundary and held to it, he was angry at first, and he later started to better recognize the damaging behavior patterns. Our dates improved in wonderful ways.

This experience also helped me find greater self-worth as I recognized my own patterns of accepting poor behavior, and I changed my responses to those situations. After all, I am a daughter of God, and He wants me to be treated with love and respect. I can't force anyone to treat me in such ways, but I can choose to remove myself from their presence if they choose otherwise.

Committing to the truth, even if it is painful, is a critical step. We cannot change what we cannot see.

Assignment should you choose:
Consider frequently praying that Heavenly Father will help you live in truth.

Chapter 10: A Commitment to the Truth

Why Do I Need to Know the Ugly Truth?

Here is some beautiful doctrine: "And ye shall know the truth, and the truth shall make you free" (John 8:32).

I know it can be hard to face the truth about patterns of sexual betrayal. But I have also found it to be necessary.

After I walked out of our full therapeutic disclosure, I was shocked and felt like some of my innocence had been stripped away. Also, what I had learned was essential because the truth empowered me to make different and better choices.

Sometimes we think we need to learn all the details about our loved one's acting-out behaviors. This can be a fine line to walk. We do need enough information to protect ourselves, but we also don't want to invite unnecessary thoughts that might lead to trauma and PTSD-type symptoms.

My personal fit is that I don't generally want to know details that paint a picture that will traumatize me later. I do, however, want and need enough general information to know the truth about my situation. For instance, I do want to know when there have been slips with pornography. However, details such as hair color can cause my thinking to spin and make it difficult for me to not obsess about specifics.

I like the boundary of my friend who asks general questions: Who was involved? What was the acting-out behavior? Where did the acting-out behavior take place? How was the behavior accessed?

Another beautiful blessing from my husband's willingness to strive for honesty during a full therapeutic disclosure and later a polygraph disclosure was that he let me in on some of his darkest secrets and most painful experiences. He seemed genuinely surprised that I still loved him after he let me know those things. I have found that most women are willing to stay with a spouse who is actively working toward repentance.

Those struggling with compulsions or addictions often hide because of shame. Letting a spouse into those painful and dark parts and then accepting our love, compassion, and empathy can be a healing experience for individuals and for marriages that can lead to repairing damaged connections. In my own situation, hard but crucial conversations created an intimacy that had not previously been available in our marriage.

> Do you need more information in order to make more informed choices, establish a deeper connection with your spouse, or for some other reason? If so, what information might help you? What information might be damaging for you?

STAGE 3

SELF-REFINEMENT

11

The Delight of Self-Refinement

When someone suffers from sexual betrayal, some of the first messages they need to hear are these: This isn't your fault. You are more than enough. You aren't alone. There are tools that can help. (And maybe here's some chocolate.) Depending on the severity of how their experiences were internalized, these might be the main messages that someone needs to hear for months or even years.

When that severe pain calms down and emotions are better regulated, it might be time to take a look in the mirror. Some of the most beautiful healing happens when we can shift into a self-reflective mindset.

In the ancient Americas—after mountains had been moved, entire cities had been sunk into the earth, and at least one city was burned—the Savior's voice was heard throughout the land. One of the things that He said was this: "O all ye that are spared because ye were more righteous than they, will ye now return unto me, and repent of your sins, and be converted, that I may heal you?" (3 Nephi 9:13).

Those who were "more righteous" still needed to repent, change, and become better. That's part of being human. I am linking arms with you, sister, because I am as human as they get.

Humility, Honesty, Accountability, and Willingness to Connect for Sexually Betrayed Spouses

When learning about boundaries, we learned about the importance of evaluating our spouse's behavior through the lens of humility, honesty, accountability, and a willingness to connect. Those same measuring sticks can also be used for us.

Have you ever experienced a difficult situation and then afterward your mind spun in circles trying to figure out what you should or should not have done? I know I have. My best way to evaluate my part is to take a step back and look at if I was being humble, honest, accountable, and willing to connect.

> Think of a recent experience that was difficult. While thinking about that situation, reflect and write about how you did well at having the following attributes or how you would like to improve:
>
> Humble
> Honest
> Accountable
> Willing to connect (if that feels safe)

Willing to Connect with a Spouse after Sexual Betrayal

After experiencing sexual betrayal, figuring out connection with a spouse can be a muddy endeavor. At times, it is appropriate to place boundaries on connection until the reestablishment of safety is at least well under way.

When safety is established, there comes a point where we need to shift back into connection if we are planning on remaining in the marriage.

It is critical that we look at our motives for withholding emotional and physical connection. If the motive for not connecting is because safety has not been reestablished, then boundaries are likely appropriate. However, if our motives are punitive or controlling, then we need to reevaluate ourselves.

It is important to remember that we are hoping for a wonderful marriage someday. When safety is established, we need to do our part to create a joyful connection with our spouse.

Sometimes a gated approach toward connection is a good idea. For instance, if there has been a boundary in place to not go on dates, then maybe starting with a single date and seeing how that goes would be a place to start. Reconnecting might start with a conversation about desiring to move back into connection.

> *Do you feel like safety has been reestablished with your spouse? Why or why not?*
>
> *Would it feel safe to move into some form of connection? Why or why not?*
>
> *If it does feel safe to reconnect with your spouse in some way, is there some connection you might start with? Maybe even a conversation about connection?*

A Grateful Heart

A couple of years ago, I found myself in the fetal position on my bedroom floor, gasping for air and begging Heavenly Father to intervene. My husband had relapsed, was suffering from severe mental illness (which had yet to be diagnosed), and was hospitalized for suicidal issues. The threat of being a widow under such severe circumstances was terrifying and heart-wrenching, and emotional pain was additionally exacerbating my physical state.

A couple of times in the past, Heavenly Father had truly dried my tears and stood me on my feet. I was hoping for that sort of miracle, but this time proved different. As I pleaded for this sort of miraculous intervention, I felt the distinct impression that He was saying to me, "I want you to be grateful for this." I was so shocked that my flow of sobs stopped momentarily.

I thought, "Grateful? For possible suicide? For my husband lying to me and others for so long? Grateful that he painted me terribly to several people when I had done my best to advocate for him? Thankful for significant patterns of pornography use and masturbation . . . again?"

And yet I knew I had heard correctly.

You know when you try something and it's more of a checklist? That's how my gratitude began. For the first while, I found things to be "grateful" for, but my heart wasn't really invested.

Two weeks into my gratitude practice, something changed in me. My meager efforts of obedience were blessed as gratitude filled me from head to toe. I was immensely thankful for something: that I *knew* what real pain was and that it was changing me.

In the past, I had been prone to undermining pain for myself and others. It was far too easy to be judgmental, and I lacked genuine empathy.

Through this experience, I was being transformed from the inside out because of this severe trial. The new level of excruciating pain was so intense that it had taken my breath away, *and it did change me*. I better understood the Savior and recognized how He had responded to me in times of heartache. I better learned what my baptismal covenants are and more fully learned what it means to "mourn with those that mourn" and to "comfort those that stand in need of comfort" (Mosiah 18:9).

I was learning, changing, and healing. And I was absolutely grateful to learn important eternal lessons.

1 Thessalonians 5:18 says, "In *everything* give thanks, for this is the will of God in Christ Jesus concerning you" (emphasis added). We can find things to be grateful for both in good times and in times of pain, though finding gratitude in times of pain can obviously prove to be more of a challenge.

My personal experience of finding gratitude in an extreme circumstance plays a large role in why I am writing this book—because gratitude helped me find healing in unexpected and powerful ways. One of my greatest trials helped to qualify me for things that I didn't know I wanted or needed. Super cool.

> *Can you find something to be authentically grateful for in your current circumstance? Why, specifically, are you grateful?*

Gratitude Tips

Here are a few tips regarding making gratitude meaningful:

- It's important to not undermine the severity of circumstances with gratitude. Denial flourishes in such environments.
- Finding things we are authentically grateful for is crucial. For instance, in my own situation, instead of saying, "I am so glad that my husband has a sexual addiction," I might say, "I am so grateful that I have learned a lot because my husband struggles with sexual addiction."
- Using the word *and* instead of *but* can help facilitate a grateful heart. The word *but* can dismiss the first thing that was said. Consider the following sentence, "I am hurting, *and* I am grateful that with the Savior I can find what I need to heal." Both things matter.
- Intentionally practice *authentic* gratitude daily. Perhaps with a gratitude journal?
- Look for small things. For instance, someone once shared that he and his wife were in the middle of a very barren desert when she found delight in a tiny flower. He said that she could find beauty most anywhere. Actively looking in crevices and dark spots for our own "flowers" can help us find joy amid great pain.
- Zoom out of hard experiences. It is easy to focus on issues and to replay them over and over with the hope of finding a solution. Zooming out and looking at the entire picture of what our lives are allows us to see a whole picture. Typically, not everything is broken, even if it might seem that way sometimes.

Is there a gratitude practice you might like to adopt?

Blessings of Compensation

It can seem incredibly unfair to have "done all the right things" only to then feel like we are receiving a rather painful and undeserved outcome. I get it.

Elder D. Todd Christofferson addressed this when he said, "We ought not to think of God's plan as a cosmic vending machine where we (1) select a desired blessing, (2) insert the required sum of good works, and (3) the order is promptly delivered."[39]

My favorite way to shift out of a "cosmic vending machine" mindset is to look for blessings of compensation. Blessings of compensation are woven throughout my story, and they are woven throughout yours as well.

Elder Joseph B. Wirthlin said, "The Lord compensates the faithful for every loss. That which is taken away from those who love the Lord will be added unto them in His own way. While it may not come at the time we desire, the faithful will know that every tear today will eventually be returned a hundredfold with tears of rejoicing and gratitude."[40]

Now *there's* some hope.

Romans 8:28 also addresses the law of compensation: "And we know that all things work together for good to them that love God, to them who are the called according to his purpose."

Pain often becomes sacred when we seek out and find gratitude for how it has transformed us, and hope can find birth when we zoom out and intently seek God's hand in our lives. His hand is often manifested through blessings of compensation.

Blessings of compensation surround us.

My Own Blessings of Compensation

What does the principle of compensation look like exactly? Well, that varies from person to person. For example, Sister Kristin M. Yee said, "The Lord has sent me compensatory blessings. . . . He has sent mentors into my life, and sweetest and most transformative of all has been my relationship with my Heavenly Father. Through Him, I have gratefully known the gentle, protective, and perfect love of a Father."[41]

I don't know how blessings of compensation are manifested in your life, so I'll share a few ways they manifest in mine.

---

39. D. Todd Christofferson, "Our Relationship with God," *Liahona*, May 2022, 78.
40. Joseph B. Wirthlin, "Come What May and Love It," *Ensign* or *Liahona*, Nov. 2008, 28.
41. Kristin M. Yee, "Beauty for Ashes: The Healing Path of Forgiveness," *Liahona*, Nov. 2022, 37.

For instance, because I could not see with my eyes what was going on, the Lord compensated my spiritual senses as I turned to Him. I have learned a great deal about walking in a blindfolded state with the Holy Ghost as my guide.

Also, because for many years I didn't understand the value of turning to earthly beings for support, I instead turned to my Heavenly Father, pouring out my soul for hours at a time over several years. This forged a relationship with Him that is priceless to me, and I actively invest in this relationship to this day.

Another blessing of compensation is that I had preconceived ideas about parenting that have been challenged. Due to this newfound awareness, I am practicing skills that allow me to better emotionally connect with my children in meaningful ways, ways in which I was not capable of previously.

I have had to look at myself long and hard in the mirror, deciding who I am and who I want to be. This has been defining and empowering in many ways. Due to this process, I am practicing being compassionate to myself and others and am developing other character traits that I hope to bring with me into the next life.

Another blessing of compensation is that I previously did not know how to sit with others who were hurting without trying to fix their pain. My trials have taught me much about that, and I now take that covenant and responsibility very seriously. I now show up differently in this world, and because of that, I have been blessed to experience many deep and meaningful relationships over the last few years. Such relationships once eluded me and were a mystery.

After years of actively looking for the blessings of compensation that the Lord has graciously given to me, I have decided I don't want to give them back. Even though the price has been severe at times, I would pay it again. This does not mean that I am glad to have suffered through patterns of sexual betrayal and other major trials. But it does mean that I recognize the compensation to be more than fair.

Seeking out blessings of compensation has been a light in times of darkness in my life. As Elder David A. Bednar taught, "I joyfully witness that compensating blessings will come as we strive to fulfill our individual responsibility to learn and love the restored gospel of Jesus Christ."[42]

> What are some of the blessings of compensation in your life?

Service Through Sharing Your Experience, Faith, and Hope

Sexual betrayal usually touches nearly every insecure place in those of us who experience it. No one chooses to be sexually betrayed.

One blessing of compensation for those of us who grasp on to recovery is that we eventually find great joy in what we learn and in who we are becoming. It can seem ironic that trials can bring out the best in us, and yet it's true. As you heal and become, others will need to know what you have paid the price to learn. They will need your experience, faith, and hope.

Many people have allowed me the privilege of standing on their shoulders. They let me see ahead, so to speak, and by so doing, I have been able to move through similar paths with greater ease. In a similar fashion, I am saying to you, "I have been down a similar path. I'll share some of the light that helped me to see better."

And the same can be true for you when you have received the necessary understanding and healing. You will be able to turn around and grab the hand of the next person as you help pull them to higher ground, and the Savior will smile as you do this.

That seems to be how the Savior works much of the time. He helps us directly or seemingly indirectly, and then He hopes we will pass on the baton.

Here's a really cool blessing of compensation that happens when we turn around and lift others: sharing our own experience, faith, and hope can expedite and strengthen *our* recovery as well. It acts as a beautiful circle that comes back around to bless and strengthen us.

There are many ways to minister to others in the realm of sexual betrayal. A few of my friends have let their bishops know that they struggle

---

42. David A. Bednar, "Prepared to Obtain Every Needful Thing," *Ensign* or *Liahona*, May 2019, 104.

with sexual betrayal and have given their bishops permission to pass on their names to women in their wards who have experienced similar things. For those who attend recovery meetings, there are often many opportunities to connect with heartbroken sisters. Some women have blogged anonymously, while others feel called to share more publicly. Sometimes heaven places women in our path who we can heal with and minister to individually.

There is no right or wrong way to minister to and connect with others. When we look for opportunities to serve, eventually paths open up.

The Lord qualifies us through trials to serve in new and perhaps even more meaningful ways. None of us wants to be qualified, because the refiner's fire is incredibly hot. But the qualification process, while painful, can become a sacred blessing.

> How and when might you like to share your experience, faith, and hope with others?

In the Service of God by Lifting Others

Years ago, I sat pondering over Mosiah 2:17: "When ye are in the service of your fellow beings ye are only in the service *of your God*" (emphasis added). What does it mean that we are in the service *of our God?* Why does our service affect *Him* so deeply and directly?

To bring this concept into a real-life scenario, let's suppose that you brought a friend dinner when they were sick. Because of that act of service, that person felt loved, they were able to receive more needed rest, and they did not have to spend time and energy cooking and cleaning.

Did that act of service help your friend? Of course it did. And isn't it possible that it helped the Savior to feel some relief as well?

Christ also taught this principle:

> For I was an hungred, and ye gave me meat: I was thirsty, and ye gave me drink: I was a stranger, and ye took me in:
> Naked, and ye clothed me: I was sick, and ye visited me: I was in prison, and ye came unto me.
> Then shall the righteous answer him, saying, Lord, when saw we thee an hungred, and fed *thee?* or thirsty, and gave *thee* drink?

When saw we thee a stranger, and took *thee* in? or naked, and clothed *thee*?

Or when saw we thee sick, or in prison, and came unto thee?

And the King shall answer and say unto them, Verily I say unto you, Inasmuch as ye have done *it* unto one of the least of these my brethren, *ye have done it unto me*. (Matthew 25:35–40; emphasis added)

Ringing in my heart are the Savior's words, *"Ye have done it unto me."*

At times, I have been incredibly concerned that the Savior suffered for me. Didn't He suffer enough to not add *my* sins and heartache to those great drops of blood?

Redemptive to that concept is that the Savior says that we serve *Him* when we lift the burdens of others.

Walking through patterns of sexual betrayal from a spouse can qualify us to be the Savior's hands in unique ways. We can deliver messages of hope that others are starving for. We lift up weary hands and strengthen feeble knees. We will be able to testify of ways He has lifted our burdens.

Now consider this with me: what relief might the Savior feel when you reach out to and console those who have experienced similar things in your circle?

Ministering with Humility

When I share hard things with my dear friend and sponsor in the 12-step program for sexual betrayal, she often generously says, "It helps me too." When she says this, my heart always seems to let out a sigh of relief because I don't feel like a burden.

A few years ago, the Spirit nearly yelled at me to start a podcast regarding sexual betrayal. I pushed back when I said, "I will definitely do that . . . in three to four years when I have healed from this mess." The Spirit replied, *"Now."* Sharing my story and my limited experience was a scary endeavor, and while I strove for humility, I lacked it in many ways during this period of time. This was due in large part because I felt chosen. And I *was* chosen, just not as I had suspected. My podcast was to be an opportunity for me to learn and grow. There were concepts that I needed to be sealed in my heart. I thought I was called because I knew things, but I came to see that I was actually called because I needed to learn more.

I have since shifted and continue to practice shifting from my prideful stance. I genuinely believe that, like everyone else, I sometimes share things that I have learned *and* I love to soak in what I learn from others. I am genuinely curious about what I can learn from most anyone. I see each of the women I meet as having things to benefit my own learning and growth, no matter where they are on their path to recovery. I take delight in repeating my sponsor's words to friends who reach out by sometimes saying, "It helps me too."

The interesting thing is that as I have shifted in this way, my support community has grown in large ways. Loneliness has been replaced with overflowing support, connection, and love. I attribute this growth to God as He has helped me learn to lay down my desire to control. Heavenly Father has helped me strive to value connection over being right, and I better soak in what others have to offer.

When we can shift in humble ways, which usually requires intervention from the Savior, other people better sense that they are safe with us. And safe connection feels so good.

> *What areas in your life might benefit from you practicing greater humility?*

The 12 Steps

I believe strongly that everyone has their own path to healing and that the Savior works in stunning ways with whatever He inspires us to do. I am briefly addressing 12 Steps here in case it might be a good option for some, as it has been a wonderful blessing in my own life.

I love 12 Steps and find that it brings me closer to God, helps me find accountability for my actions, and helps me lean into the Savior. I think the 12-step guide is actually a beautiful and divinely inspired guide to accessing the Atonement.

Steps 1–3 are amazing resources during any stage of recovery and can be repeated over and over. Steps 4–10 are more like Stage 3 work. I wasn't ready for Stage 3 work for quite a while, and if it takes you a while to be ready, that's okay.

I recommend the S.A. Lifeline 12-step program, the Healing Through Christ 12-step program, and the S-Anon 12-step program. All have meetings for spouses who have been sexually betrayed and are organized to include sponsorship, though sponsorship is generally not encouraged as strongly in the Healing Through Christ program. Sponsorship is a crucial piece of 12-step work.

Forgiveness

Forgiveness is a hard concept for some, particularly those whose lives have been significantly altered by patterns of sexual betrayal. After safety has been established, our need to forgive can often be assessed more objectively.

We absolutely want to be able to lay grudges, bitterness, and hatred at the feet of the Savior. Forgiveness frees us from carrying the weight of past hurts and burdens. When we are able to truly forgive, we come to know, in personal ways, that His yoke is easy and His burden really is light (see Matthew 11:28–30).

Forgiveness can also be a journey instead of a destination. Sometimes we can quickly forgive, and other times it can be a process. Sister Kristin M. Yee said, "The timing of that healing is individual and we cannot judge another's timing. It is important to allow ourselves the necessary time to heal and to be kind to ourselves in the process."[43]

How to actually forgive is an incredibly personal endeavor because what we truly need is a new heart. While a new heart is something we can work toward, it is ultimately a gift from the Savior. When we offer Him our soft hearts, He can plant seeds that grow—seeds like forgiveness (see Matthew 13:8).

The Savior understands what will illuminate each step of our path toward forgiveness. The process helps us develop a deeper relationship with Him plus a greater personal understanding of the Atonement.

Safety and Forgiveness

Forgiveness is often one of the first things that good-intentioned souls preach to sexually betrayed spouses. It is also a principle we commonly beat ourselves up with. Forgiveness is certainly a commandment and a critical one at that. But it's also frequently misunderstood, and it can feel more like a weapon when taught in inappropriate ways.

The basic concept of well-intentioned advice regarding forgiveness often stems from the thought that if betrayed spouses could only forgive, we

---

43. Kristin M. Yee, "Beauty for Ashes," 38.

would no longer feel hurt. This can be true for some things and false for others.

Feeling anger, for instance, can sometimes tell us that a great injustice has occurred and safety is being compromised. If we look at such a situation through the lens that forgiveness will solve the issue, then we completely miss the fact that when safety is compromised, a boundary is needed. A lack of safety creates powerful emotions that act as warnings. Misjudging these warnings as needing to forgive can perpetuate patterns of compulsions, addictions, and even abuse.

Let's return to the Lord turning over tables in the temple for an example of this. Jesus was rightfully angry, and no one counseled Him to simply forgive the moneychangers. That perfect Son of God, being the most divine example to ever walk this earth, created a boundary when He used anger in a way that created change. His actions in the temple that day are frequently marveled at over two millennia later.

Those who advocate for forgiveness when the issue is one of safety unintentionally miss the mark with their counsel. It is important to recognize this well-meaning yet destructive misunderstanding because if we don't create safety when patterns of sexual betrayal and sometimes abuse are present, we are bound to be acted upon in damaging ways. In such instances, it may be important to let God prevail by recognizing that although the person offering said counsel has greatness of heart in their favor, there is a fundamental misunderstanding in their interpretation of doctrine. We can thank them for their opinion and genuine concern for us and then focus on the issue of creating safety with different support.

When we strive to be forgiving by enduring patterns of behavior that create a great lack of safety, we often end up being treated in ways that are not pleasing to our Heavenly Father. We rarely help our loved ones by suffering through destructive patterns. Those types of efforts on our part can even enable increasingly worse behavior.

Trust and forgiveness are not the same things. Forgiveness is a gift, and trust needs to be earned. If trust is restored too quickly after patterns of sexual betrayal have been present, then it is very likely we will live through similar injuries on repeat. Offering trust too soon is not helpful for the salvation of individual souls and can even impede the exaltation of families.

Forgiveness also does not mean that we need to continue to be in close proximity with a person who causes significant pain by their actions or non-actions. Sister Kristin M. Yee said, "Please know that forgiving someone does not mean that you put yourself in a position where you will continue to be hurt. 'We can work toward forgiving someone and still feel prompted by the Spirit to stay away from them.'"[44]

Let's revisit Joseph in Egypt with more attention to detail. There is often a lot of mention that Joseph was incredibly forgiving of his brothers, and he certainly was that. What we don't hear much about is Joseph's journey with forgiveness. Was it instant? Was it a process? Did he wrestle with God over such things before he could see a zoomed-out view of heaven's plan for him and his family?

When Joseph's brothers left to go home and bring back Benjamin, what was Joseph's experience like during that period? Was his heart softened toward forgiveness then, was he forgiving from the time he was sold, or something else?

I wish we had more insight into those twenty-two years because sometimes forgiveness is a process and can be an ongoing wrestle with God. I have never heard scripture say that we have to forgive "instantly." What if forgiveness is more of a journey for many of us than an event? To me, God values my effort, and He has yet to expect my perfection. If I am actively working at forgiving, I believe those efforts are enough.

Going back to Joseph, let's remember that he did seem to separate trust from forgiveness. Part of this included Joseph engineering a plan to have his brothers bring Benjamin back to Egypt. As you likely remember, Benjamin was the youngest brother who was well loved by their father, Jacob. After the loss of Joseph, Jacob's sons watched their father grieve and mourn in devastating ways for twenty-two years. When Benjamin came to Egypt, Joseph framed him for theft and insisted that Benjamin remain to be his servant. After this came a great thing of importance for Joseph to see: his brothers showed genuine humility. Judah and the other brothers "fell before him on the ground" (Genesis 44:14). Judah begged and pleaded with Joseph for mercy, and he even offered to take Benjamin's place as Joseph's servant.

Then something miraculous happened. Joseph started sobbing after this display of humility, and trust began to be reestablished. Joseph "could not refrain himself," and he stood before his brothers and revealed himself. It is evident that Joseph truly had forgiven his brothers because he said and

---

44. Kristin M. Yee, "Beauty for Ashes," 37.

did beautiful things. For instance, he said, "Be not grieved, nor angry with yourselves, that ye sold me hither: for God did send me before you to preserve life. . . . God sent me before you to preserve you a posterity in the earth and to save your lives by a great deliverance. So now it was not you that sent me hither, but God" (Genesis 45:5, 7–8).

Joseph of Egypt is an amazing example that after safety has been established—which is based in humility, honesty, accountability, and a willingness to connect—it is much simpler to see what we need to forgive.

Can you see the difference between forgiveness and trust in your own situation?

12
Learning to Have a Voice

Empowerment is a critical part of healing from destructive patterns. As human beings, we have each been wounded and we are all healing. What we say and how we say it often reflects that level of healing. We have all said things in a wounded state, and the results are often more pain and heartache. While we can and should offer ourselves self-compassion for such responses, we are each responsible to engage in our own healing.

Empowerment from a place of healing has much greater influence and can connect others in incredible ways. I like to use the term "righteous empowerment" to describe the empowerment that comes from healing and the strengthening power of the Atonement.

Healing can produce feelings of righteous empowerment. When this is the case, the fruits are often that we stand in humble confidence in who we are and the inspired messages that the Spirit has commanded us to share. We do so without shrinking or puffing up. We see the good in others and in ourselves while standing firm in truth.

Even though I haven't generally pointed out where righteous empowerment is in this book, I'll name a few concepts:

- Making our own decisions that are based on personal revelation is empowering.
- It can be empowering to come to understand our worth to God and how we should be treated.

- Coming to understand that we are responsible for our emotions is empowering.
- Boundaries are an empowering concept and help us not be subject to another person's destructive patterns.
- Making decisions based on truth is also an empowering concept.
- The healing process is also empowering because we act differently when we are healed.

Another way to experience righteous empowerment is to learn to use our voices in respectful and meaningful ways while standing firm in truth.

> *In what ways do you feel righteous empowerment in your own situation?*
>
> *Is there a form of righteous empowerment that you might like to practice and develop more fully?*

Heaven Is Organized in Families, and Why That Matters for Finding Our Voices

Elder L. Tom Perry said, "We believe that the organization and government of heaven will be built around families and extended families."[45]

Isn't it interesting that while we are organized into wards, branches, stakes, and areas on the earth, it's the patriarchal order that prevails in heaven? Heaven is organized into families. This is critical to know because when we go to the temple and enter into the new and everlasting covenant, we have eternal responsibilities to our families.

Sometimes it's hard to know what to say, what our role is, and if it's appropriate to speak up and speak out. As wives, sisters, daughters, and mothers in Zion, we have a great invested interest in what happens to our families. Who on this earth is better qualified to advocate for our eternal families than we are? Likely no one.

---

45. L. Tom Perry, "Why Marriage and Family Matter—Everywhere in the World," *Ensign* or *Liahona*, May 2015, 41.

President Nelson said about women, "Your participation is essential and never ornamental!"[46] He also said, "We need your strength, your conversion, your conviction, your ability to lead, your wisdom, and your voices."[47]

While we cannot control outcomes, we can hope, learn, teach, and advocate for a brighter future. Using our voices in effective ways is the essence of pioneering such efforts. What we say and how we say it has the potential to bless generations to come.

You might ask, "Who am I to speak up?"

Gently pushing back, I ask you: Who are you to not speak truthfully about things that might affect your eternity?

To stand our sacred ground in truth can be a holy endeavor. We can become empowered as daughters of God, standing firm in our identity as rightful heirs in His kingdom. What we have to say is generally not frivolous and can have ripple effects for generations. When we use our voices without controlling, especially when we feel guided by the Holy Ghost, we find genuine worth and belonging in the kingdom of God. This does not mean that everyone will agree with what we share, but it does mean that we can have great internal peace that we have done as our Father in Heaven has asked and that we have done our best to advocate for our families.

> *What comes to mind when you ask yourself, "Who am I to speak up?" (No answer is right or wrong.)*

What Is in Our Purview

It's important to recognize what we can do and what we should not do. Elder Dale G. Renlund said, "We receive personal revelation only within our purview and not within the prerogative of others."[48] I have stewardship for myself, for my family, in my calling under the keys of priesthood holders, and to use my voice as revealed in ways that don't include control.

---

46. Russell M. Nelson, "Spiritual Treasures," *Ensign* or *Liahona*, May 2019, 79.
47. Russell M. Nelson, "A Plea to My Sisters," *Ensign* or *Liahona*, Nov. 2015, 95.
48. Dale G. Renlund, "A Framework for Personal Revelation," *Liahona*, Nov. 2022, 16.

For instance, when decisions and actions of authority figures have the potential to affect my eternal family, I believe that using my voice in truthful, respectful, and inspired ways is within my purview. What is not within my purview is how the leader acts and responds to what I have said.

We need to be very careful that we do not use control in any way when we act on such promptings. For instance, I would not go on a strike of sorts to encourage the leader to make a different decision. I should not demand or demean, and while I can suggest outcomes, if they decide on a different path, I need to respect that they are acting within their purview.

While I can voice things that I am prompted to say, the leader also has the responsibility to receive revelation and to act according to their own revelation.

My faith needs to be in my Savior and not in my own desired outcome.

Surrendering Outcomes and Honoring Agency

After acting on revelation, sometimes it's easy to think, "I was inspired to say and do these things. Why was there not a better outcome?"

That can definitely be confusing. I have decided that the Savior must know something in those situations that I am not aware of. Perhaps acting on inspiration was the planting of one seed out of many. Also, we might not be afforded the opportunity to hear conversations behind closed doors. Another possibility is that the other person might be inspired to go in a different direction altogether. The person might also not be responding via revelation at all, and we cannot make them choose otherwise. We don't get to choose the outcome and should not try to control other people to achieve our desired outcome.

We won't always know why, but when we let God prevail, we speak when He prompts us to do so and surrender the outcomes that we cannot control.

Again, we need to have faith in the Savior and not in the desired outcome.

> *In your own situation, where might your faith be in the Savior and where might your faith be in outcomes?*

Chapter 12: Learning to Have a Voice

It's Going to Be Messy and Why That's Okay

In an ideal world, communicating in effective ways is best accomplished when we have a level of awareness, healing, tools, empathy, and understanding. However, optimal circumstances are not always available to us.

It is important to remember that when we engage in difficult conversations in imperfect ways, it is courageous to try regardless of the outcome. I have decided that when using my voice about things that are important, it is better that I strive and sometimes fall short than to not try at all. When I inevitably fall short in my communication, it is a good opportunity for me to evaluate what I did well and in what areas I would like to improve.

Thankfully, the Savior seems much more invested in growth than He is with my imperfections, which is a melt-worthy element of grace. The Savior gets it like no one else can. Not only does He understand why I imperfectly communicate at times, but He loves me still and celebrates my progress.

When we try something new, like communicating effectively about agonizingly painful things, there are bound to be mistakes, and that's okay. With ample self-compassion, we can evaluate our role, be accountable for things we would like to do differently, repair what we can, and try again another time. Progress over perfection.

Learning to Use Our Voices During Important Conversations in Marriage

Let's start out by validating that it's often a painful and difficult endeavor to learn to communicate effectively with our spouse after sexual betrayal. The one we would normally turn to is the very one who broke our hearts. Learning to communicate effectively after significant breaches in trust can be arduous.

Add to the confusion that compulsions and addictions can literally change the brain of the user and that the brain often needs to physically heal in order to have reasonable conversations.

Some of the following concepts may or may not apply to the period of time immediately following discovery or disclosure. Also, different circumstances require personal adjustment. I will share things to consider with God.

Prior to sitting down to partake of a meal, we set the table. Let's also practice "setting the table" for important conversations with our spouse after experiencing sexual betrayal. Here are a few ideas:

- Before engaging in difficult marital conversations, it's important to strive to find emotional stability in ourselves. The only person someone can control is their own self, which gives us the responsibility to meet those needs as best as we can, preferably before hard conversations. Sometimes finding emotional stability might require participating in soul-care of some kind.
- Another way to prepare for conversations is to remember that timing is critical. For instance, I am prone to being grouchy at night, while my husband is much less cheerful in the morning. Perhaps an afternoon conversation might be better?
- Also, if I spring a hard conversation on my husband without warning, things are much less likely to go well. When people have a heads-up to find emotional stabilization first, conversations sometimes go better. For instance, I might first say, "I would really like to talk about what happened last night. Could we maybe set up a time to talk about that?"
- When a spouse has not yet developed honesty, reminding oneself of the truth beforehand can help. Compulsions and addictions often create confusion and chaos. It can be difficult to stay firm in the truth when manipulative and destructive things are being thrown our way. Grounding in truth before hard conversations can help us stay present when faced with confusion and chaos. Perhaps making our own list of the facts and reviewing them before the conversation can help us stay focused.
- Remaining curious is also a critical skill to practice. When we stay curious with our loved ones, conversations are much less threatening. Also, we are able to stay in the reasoning part of our brains, which helps us communicate more effectively and with greater emotional stability. An example of staying curious might be by saying, "When you view pornography, the story I tell myself is that I am not enough for you. Is that true?"
- Being honest about our experiences and emotions can help our loved ones develop empathy. So many of us try to save our loved

ones from witnessing the severe pain we go through. This is not generally helpful in their recovery process, and it can be a good thing for them to learn to see our genuine pain. Also, though, if they are not capable of being empathetic, we may need to get that validation and support elsewhere.
- Consider the previously mentioned template for boundaries from the Garden of Eden during hard conversations. For instance, I might say, "I would really like to have this conversation, and in order to do that, I need honesty and kindness. I can continue in this conversation when and if you are able to be honest and kind."

If either spouse becomes emotionally flooded during such conversations, then perhaps set up a time to revisit the subject. If similar results occur, consider meeting with a qualified therapist as a third party.

> *How might you consider "setting the table" for hard conversations with your loved one?*

About First Responders for Sexual Betrayal

I share the following with great love and compassion plus a commitment to the truth. Many "first responders" who strive to help sexually betrayed spouses (such as therapists and priesthood leaders) have yet to be afforded the necessary understanding and training to fulfill such roles in effective and compassionate ways. It's kind of like a paramedic who has yet to learn how to splint a leg or apply pressure to stop the bleeding. There is generally no ill will in this lack of understanding.

In the therapy world, for instance, treating sexual betrayal is a relatively new field that is still being studied. While some therapists have the appropriate understanding, experience, and training to help a sexually betrayed spouse, many do not—at least not yet. Accessibility to beautiful resources is gratefully improving. But until the expansion of appropriate resources infiltrates a majority of the understanding in first responders, we are not simply left to the mercy of others. We can become educated in these subjects and learn how to use our voices in kind and effective ways. In a way, *we* can become first responders who Christ qualifies to help weary souls who are affected by patterns of sexual betrayal.

When first responders learn how to do things better, they are much more effective, and I believe they will be more effective in the future. Until then, it is imperative that we speak up when further harm is caused.

I will pass on to you what my good friend Katy Willis said to me a few years ago: "It will take many voices to make a difference." It is easy to not recognize the significance of one voice, but several voices crying out are more easily heard and understood.

Your voice may or may not make a difference in your own situation, but I do believe that using your voice in effective ways has great potential to help others in the future, perhaps even those of your own posterity.

Finding Your Voice with Church Leaders

A line in the Church's ARP support guide for family members says this: "When speaking with Church leaders, be mindful that, because leaders have different levels of knowledge, it may be necessary to help them understand what we are going through."[49] I want to validate that this is a tall order for some of us, especially when experiencing strong emotions. I also offer my hope that a large part of this burden can hopefully be lifted off the shoulders of sexually betrayed spouses, largely by awareness training for Church leadership. Until then, we can practice finding kind and effective ways to share the seriousness of our situations with leaders.

As we navigate hard conversations, it's important to remember that each human being is subject to the Fall. This means that no one can possibly offer perfect counsel. If God is at my center, then letting God prevail includes double-checking counsel with Him, especially counsel that doesn't feel quite right. Oftentimes, that uncomfortable feeling might be a warning from the Holy Ghost.

None of this means that Church leadership should be treated disrespectfully or that they should be disregarded. On the contrary, the Church is organized on the earth to include structure, callings, and priesthood mantles. Such things do matter, but so does a remembrance that all people fall short in understanding. As mortals, we are all subject to the Fall; therefore, let *God* prevail.

---

49. *Support Guide: Help for Spouses and Family of Those in Recovery* (2017), 36.

Chapter 12: Learning to Have a Voice

Because understanding the effects of sexual betrayal and sexual compulsions and addictions is in its infancy, our generation is made up of pioneers of sorts. We are doing the hard work of walking in the wilderness without a trail. Make no mistake—others will see the wheel-worn grass. As we pull our handcarts, it will be easier for future generations.

It is important to remember what we can control and what we cannot control. For instance, we can control what we say and how we say it, as directed by the Holy Ghost. We can share our own experiences and what we have learned. We can also make requests. However, we cannot control what Church leaders say and do. Such efforts at control cross over into not honoring agency.

How the Message Is Delivered Matters

I learned the hard way that no matter how correct the message is, how I say it may be even more important. A while ago, this was a skill that I had yet to learn, and I was about to be thrown into the real-world laboratory.

I had lived for the past four years with my husband being an emotional time bomb that would often explode, usually without provocation. Our entire family had suffered in severe ways. I couldn't put my finger on the issue until the Spirit guided me to evidence that my husband had been looking at pornography . . . again.

I remember thinking, "This is the root of our issues! Finally! The bishop will help me now that I have proof!"

I didn't know what trauma was at the time, I had yet to experience any recovery, and I knew very little about emotional regulation. Looking into life's rearview mirror, I see that I was definitely suffering from major trauma when my husband and I entered our bishop's office. I remember that my body was shaking, and I was incredibly distressed.

In anxious tones, I explained my husband's thirty-plus year history regarding his relationship with pornography and that it had affected our family greatly. Though I can't remember what else I said, my words were possibly strong and harsh since that was my frequent pattern when dealing with traumatic events at that point in my life.

My husband simply sat silently with his head hung low.

I distinctly remember our bishop looking at me like I was crazy. (I certainly felt crazy.) He then sent me into the hall while he talked with my husband for a couple of hours.

When I was invited back into his office to rejoin them, the bishop said something like "I have talked to Bart, and he's confessed." Then with a big smile on his face, he said, "Good news! He can now take the sacrament and go to the temple."

I felt like I had been punched in the gut. I remember thinking, "Will no one help my family?!"

When we returned home, my husband used the bishop's words of forgiveness to suggest that I needed to just forgive and forget. After all, the Savior forgave him, so I needed to as well. In his mind, confessing was now done and we should be able to move on.

His ideas about forgiveness and trust were obviously confused at that point. Sadly, the bishop's counsel and leniency during this visit was used by my husband as a weapon of sorts instead of as a tool for healing.

Awareness Training

My experience stands in stark contrast to a later time when my dear friend Katy Willis was invited by the stake president to offer awareness training to the bishops in our stake about helping women find healing from sexual betrayal.[50] At that point, Katy had been in recovery from sexual betrayal for several years and had invested heavily in her healing. I watched as my own good bishop listened intently to her and learned. I was fascinated because things that I had told my bishop were sometimes minimized and disregarded, but when Katy delivered similar messages, he listened closely. And he changed.

I have compassion toward our bishop, who was doing the best he knew how.

What I am going to say should not be disregarded or taken lightly: After receiving awareness training from Katy, my bishop did better in hard conversations. Much better. This information is important because people often can learn and do better when they have the right information.

Another example of how training could have helped was when I was a ward Relief Society president several years ago. During that period, I thought I had the magic key to keeping my husband's sexual addiction at

---

50. Katy Willis, "Betrayal Trauma Spiritual Support Team Training," Grace for Betrayal, accessed Oct. 27, 2022, https://graceforbetrayaltrauma.teachable.com/p/betrayal-trauma-spiritual-support-team-training.

bay by providing sex any time he wanted it, regardless of how he was treating me. I remember telling two different bishops that I was concerned for the women in our ward because it was my understanding that they were withholding sex from their husbands and, in response, their husbands were turning to pornography. (I have an awful lot of shame writing this, and if you have read this book to this point, you will see that my views have significantly evolved after receiving better education.) My uninspired advice was obviously faulty.

Please consider with me the difference it would've made in my own situation to have even some basic education about the subject of sexual compulsions and addictions. Such understanding could have possibly had a trickle-down effect and might have blessed the other sisters whom I love dearly. On a personal note, if what I said to either bishop played any part in them responding in inappropriate ways to my dear sisters, I would love to strive to make amends to them somehow.

I, therefore, continue to use my voice to request better training for Church leaders as I equally practice surrendering whether or not that training happens. I strongly believe that Church leaders desire to be effective in their roles. They are doing the best they know how, and I strongly believe that they do better when they know more about hard subjects. Just like you and me.

Remembering Pahoran in Hard Conversations

When I think of my friend Katy's talents in addressing priesthood leaders, I believe they are almost magical. I have decided that she must have spiritual gifts in safe communication. However, she also demonstrates skills. The wonderful news is that skills can be learned.

Such observations have led me to delve into my own studies about engaging in hard conversations in effective ways. Let's consider Pahoran from the Book of Mormon, who is an amazing example of modeling an excruciating conversation with an authority figure.

Captain Moroni was feeling abandoned by the government, of which Pahoran was the governor. Moroni and his army were fighting for just causes, like family, freedom to worship, liberty, and even their very lives. Their army was not receiving much-needed supplies, food, or additional men to fight. His people were dying in battle, and Moroni . . . well, he was angry.

Livid would actually be a better description for how he was feeling. And maybe even hangry, but I digress.

Not knowing the circumstances Pahoran was in, Moroni lashed out and said things like "I have somewhat to say unto them by way of condemnation" (Alma 60:2), "Great has been your neglect towards us" (Alma 60:5), and—my personal favorite—"Can you think to sit upon your thrones in a state of thoughtless stupor?" (Alma 60:7). This was not a short lashing, as Moroni (whom I love) went on for thirty-six verses.

What Moroni did not realize was that Pahoran was also in a very severe situation. He had been kicked out of the city by the king-men, had experienced a lack of provisions himself, and felt lost as to what he could do.

Pahoran was strongly misjudged, he was unseen for the righteous desires of his heart, his circumstances were misunderstood, and he was addressed harshly regarding things well beyond his control.

A crushing reality is that as spouses who have suffered from patterns of sexual betrayal, we can sometimes be judged in similar ways.

Despite the sharp rebuke, Pahoran responded to Moroni with such graciousness that I am often amazed when I study it. After explaining the severity of his situation to Moroni, he said something incredibly generous: "You have censured me, but it mattereth not; I am not angry, but do rejoice in the greatness of your heart" (Alma 61:9). Isn't it beautiful that Pahoran saw through the harsh words and judged Moroni's amazing heart while also standing fast in the truth?

I want to be like that.

I've wondered how I could use Pahoran's example as a template when faced with a severe situation when an authority figure's faulty perspective is affecting me.

Here's my Pahoran-inspired process:

1. Remember that, ultimately, the truth comes from God. He is the filter for any counsel that is received from human beings.
2. Remember that the authority figure generally has "greatness of heart" in their favor, and they are also, like you and me, subject to the Fall.
3. Find common ground by validating the parts of truth in what they have shared.

4. Speak up in kind ways while standing firm in God-given truth, and set a boundary if necessary.

Applying a Pahoran-Inspired Process

I had the opportunity to use some of my hard-learned skills in a difficult situation a couple of years ago.

I had seen the same pattern many times. It went something like the following.

My husband would relapse for a long period of time. Our family would suffer greatly from his actions during that period, which would last years or, less frequently, months. I would know that something was wrong for a long period of time, but I couldn't quite put my finger on the issue, and he would deny any acting-out behaviors. I would eventually find evidence of a relapse and approach my husband about it. He would continue to deny participating in destructive behavior and then concede when I had enough information.

My husband would then confess to the bishop, who would see my husband in a broken state. The bishop would typically offer scriptures, conference talks, and prayer, then say something like "Thank you for your confession" and send him on his way. There would be little or no follow-up, nor accountability, even on the occasion when my husband asked for more of those things.

My husband would use their leniency in destructive ways to minimize his behavior and justify his continuation of harmful patterns.

Rinse. Repeat. *For more than twenty years.*

I do see the greatness of heart in our priesthood leaders. But I also believe that the leniency that was directed toward my husband over the years contributed to him participating in destructive patterns that greatly harmed our family.

This time, we had made it to the stage where I found evidence of a relapse, and I knew that the next step would be my husband going to see the bishop. By this point, I was bone-weary. Being married to someone in active addiction is difficult beyond words. Even still, I felt a glimmer of hope as I remembered that I could use my voice.

As I zoomed out and recognized the pattern, I wondered how I could fight for my husband and for my eternal family differently this time.

I labored in prayer and finally emerged with my own heaven-approved course of action.

With the guidance of the Holy Ghost, I decided to speak with the bishop prior to my husband visiting with him. I reminded myself often that the bishop was doing the best he knew how and that he possessed "greatness of heart" like Moroni. While speaking with the bishop, I laid out the previous pattern for him, and I asked the bishop to please do something different. I asked him to hold my husband accountable this time.

The bishop's reply was admittedly discouraging to me. He said that not much is done for compulsive pornography use in the Church, to which I found the following quote in the Church's handbook and texted it to him: "A Church membership council may be necessary if a member . . . uses pornography intensively or compulsively, causing significant harm to a member's marriage or family."[51]

While I might be judged for this response, I know that my heart was not asking for punitive compensation. I left that conversation feeling confident that my language was kind and direct during this exchange.

My bishop sent me to the stake president after our conversation. I repeated to my stake president what I had told my bishop and thought that he might choose to change the pattern. However, I was disappointed that, while my husband was called in to visit with the stake president a couple of times, my husband was ultimately sent home with his love, counsel, and a general conference talk but no further accountability.

I sustain, love, and forgive my bishop and stake president. I accept their decisions and believe in their greatness of heart while simultaneously believing that there were mistakes made. I also believe that they did the best they knew how under difficult circumstances. They are subject to the Fall just like I am. I have no control over the outcome, as it was not my decision to make.

Here is why I share this experience, even though the outcome was not as I had hoped for. I left that experience with peace that I had fought for my eternal family in a new way. I used my voice without regret regarding how I said things. With the Spirit's guidance, I was grateful to sort out what part was mine and what part was my priesthood leaders'. It felt wonderful and

---

51. *General Handbook: Serving in The Church of Jesus Christ of Latter-day Saints*, 38.6.5, ChurchofJesusChrist.org.

empowering to say things in a way that the Spirit witnessed were pleasing to my Heavenly Father. I recognized that the Savior celebrated that I had done something brave, and I have a powerful memory of Him mourning with me when the outcome was not as I had hoped for.

Even though the result wasn't as I had desired, it was still sacred.

> *Are there Pahoran-like attitudes and behaviors you might like to practice in your communication skills? If so, what are they?*

"The" Letter

While kneeling in prayer, I felt strongly that Heavenly Father had a message for me. As I listened and asked questions, I felt prompted that it wasn't about my family and it wasn't about our finances, both of which had been weighing on me. It was about the book I was writing—this book. I soon realized that Heavenly Father wanted me to include "*The* Letter." I had no intention of sharing this letter, and I do so at this time only because of personal revelation.

After sitting with many covenant-keeping women who have been unintentionally misjudged or who were unintentionally given harmful counsel from Church leaders, I felt several strong promptings to draft the following letter. Fifty-seven other women signed this letter. There would have been more, but confidentiality—which is understandably a need for some women—was not part of this letter. The letter was individually mailed to each member of the First Presidency, each member of the Quorum of the Twelve Apostles, each member of the Relief Society General Presidency, each member of the Presidency of the Seventy, and each member of the Presiding Bishopric. It read:

> Dear Beloved Brethren and Sisters,
>
> We are a group of sisters who have suffered from the sexual betrayal of someone close to us. This includes our loved ones hiding pornography use, affairs, seeking out non-relational sex, and/or many other harmful behaviors. The betrayal has come from a spouse that we have made sacred covenants with, or with whom we are considering making sacred covenants. We are all striving to keep Christ at the center of our lives and to

keep our covenants. We love the restored gospel of Jesus Christ, and we love each of you.

Please know that our intentions are not punitive in nature. As the adversary has waged this war on our families, our intentions are to fight for our families by raising awareness and to ask for additional support.

We are immensely grateful for Church leaders who are actively striving to do their best to be the Savior's hands, and we understand that with lay ministry comes challenges of various levels of understanding. It is our desire to help make the future path easier for those who suffer betrayal, for those who suffer from sexual compulsion and/or addiction, and for Church leaders that we desperately need on our support team. Please know that we are truly grateful for current and past efforts from the Church in these areas. We are also hopeful that bringing awareness to these complex issues might help.

While we believe that it is not the intent of Church leaders to cause harm, many of us have suffered greatly due to lack of education in regard to these subjects. We need the support of leaders as we fight for our families. To showcase a few of the issues that some of us have faced, we would like to share some examples; however, it is not our intent to shame leaders, nor do we wish to shame our loved ones. Bringing awareness is hopefully key to better being the Savior's hands:

- At times, the betrayed has been blamed for our loved one's sexually acting-out behaviors by Church leaders.
- Many of us have been told that if we have more sex, our issues will be resolved. Following this counsel made many of our situations worse for longer periods of time.
- When we have come to our Church leaders in great distress after a traumatizing discovery and/or confession, the distress is sometimes misjudged as the reason for our loved one's acting-out.
- Many of us have suffered physical, sexual, and/or emotional abuse by our loved ones that was minimized and/or has gone unaddressed by Church leaders.
- When we are in a traumatized/survival-type state, we sometimes receive counsel such as the betrayed needs to gain more humility, to be forgiving, to be more loving, and to be more kind, etc. While this counsel is certainly important, examples of the first things that we need to hear are that we are loved, help is available, we are not at fault for our loved one's behavior, we aren't alone, and various ways to lean into our Savior for comfort.
- Boundaries are often misunderstood by our leaders as not forgiving, even though our physical, sexual, and/or emotional safety is put into serious question without them.

- Some of our loved ones have received either great lenience or great harshness by our Church leaders.
- Sometimes leaders have counseled us and our loved ones regarding issues beyond their area of expertise.
- Many of us have been referred to Family Services for therapy when we needed a specialized therapist. Therapists without specialized training often lack the needed skills regarding these complex issues. Additionally, because Family Services provides only short-term counseling, this is often an inappropriate route.
- At times leaders have focused on repairing our marriages without thoroughly addressing the compulsive and/or addictive behaviors of our loved ones. This creates an environment in which the betrayed are expected to repair things that are often out of our control. It also places inappropriate blame on the betrayed party.
- Others have been questioned about our own worthiness in association with the behaviors of our loved ones.

We believe in continuing revelation and that you are all men and women with sacred connection to the heavens. As we share a suggestion to make this path easier, please know that we are hopeful that more awareness will help in your continuing revelation. We ultimately trust in your decisions regarding this matter.

Brethren and sisters, we are asking, as a united sisterhood, to please consider training for Church leaders (bishops, stake presidents, Relief Society presidents, elders quorum presidents, addiction recovery program missionaries, etc.). Should training be created, we are hopeful that faithful members who are qualified therapists, such as those who have obtained certifications in CSAT (Certified Sex Addiction Therapists) and/or APSATS (Association of Partners of Sex Addicts Trauma Specialists), can design such training. Our situations are needing figurative "heart surgeons," and "family doctors" often lack the necessary tools.

We have a brightness of hope that the trickle-down effects from such training can bless and perhaps even save many families.

As daughters of God, we want to be part of hope and healing to bless families, both ours and those to come. We are hopeful for more effective tools as we actively engage in this war. We have hope that the Savior has counted our tears and that they will mean something to future generations and to you, our beloved brethren and sisters, as well.

With great love and hope,

Daughters of God who are healing from sexual betrayal

I want to reemphasize this sentence from the letter: "We ultimately trust in your decisions regarding this matter." And that is the truth. Each and every one of these leaders is blessed with greatness of heart, and I don't know what path they should or should not take. That revelation is between them and the Lord.

I do know that the process of writing the letter was sacred to me. I felt loved by Heavenly Father and really seen by Him as well. It felt as though He had counted my tears, and whether or not anyone acted on what was shared, He healed some of my heart through that process. It also gave me hope that my posterity might have a more informed process someday should they need it.

13

The Lord's Secret Weapon Is You

Does Isaiah stump you sometimes too? I remember scratching my head about this verse: "And he hath made my mouth like a sharp sword; in the shadow of his hand hath he hid me, and made me a polished shaft; in his quiver hath he hid me" (Isaiah 49:2).

My mind was particularly drawn to the phrase "in his quiver hath he hid me." I wondered why the Lord's servant was hid away. And what was a quiver anyway? My searching led me to learn that a quiver was the sheath for a knife *or* a case where arrows are kept by an archer. Other versions of the Bible talk about the servant being an arrow, so let's stick with that second definition. To set up the rest of this chapter, here's my own synopsis of this.

The archer is the Lord. The arrow is the servant of the Lord who has been specifically designed, created, and shaped for a very special purpose. The arrow, or the servant, is hidden in the quiver until the Lord pulls the arrow out, aims, and releases it. Hopefully, the result is that the Holy Ghost can pierce hearts, just without the blood.

Basically, the arrow is the Lord's secret weapon that He hides until His purpose is made known. If we, therefore, liken this scripture to covenant-keeping daughters of God—who are battling with the Lord for the hearts of our husbands, children, family members, friends, and communities—the logical conclusion is that *the Lord's secret weapon is **you**.*

There Are Different Arrows

There are so many different arrows! Some are heavier, and some are very, very light. Some are created from metal, while others are plastic or wood. There are many different types of tips, and the length of an arrow also varies. The fletchings, or feathers, can also vary widely. Some arrows are created for competition, others for indoor shooting, and others for hunting.

As I've been formed and am being formed into an arrow, I can testify that this tends to be a painful experience. There have been times when it seems like I've been carved with a knife. Other times I wonder if I was actually being made from metal and am being formed in a scorching fire. The Archer has been incredibly patient with me as I have not always been as straight as He's needed me to be, and I have also resisted the creation process at times.

Being made into an arrow is much more painful when I push back on how I'm being formed, or when I tell the Archer things like "Wouldn't I be a much more effective arrow if my feathers were a different color? You know, like my friend's vibrant hues?" I have been prone to pleading with the Lord not to make me be in the heat of the refiner's fire. I have definitely complained when my rough edges were smoothed with what felt like a very sharp knife.

My formation almost always takes longer than I think it should, and inevitably, when I think that I must (finally) be straight enough for the Archer, He tends to gently see things I missed.

Dear friend, He will often be patient if and when we resist. However, submitting to the process is a much better option. Yes, it hurts. There will surely be heartache, tears, and pain. But He is the Master Archer. His purpose for you and for me is greater than our wildest dreams.

I have found that as the wife of a son of God who struggles with sexual addiction, this formation is often different than I had imagined. I thought I knew how to handle hard situations. Little did I know, I needed more understanding and tools to be shaped and formed into something much different than I once supposed.

I had done my very best and had thought that I knew what I needed in order to repair my situation. However, it's clear that I misunderstood.

I have come to see that the eternal education I am receiving at this time is forming more than an earthly being, and I strongly believe that is the case for you as well.

> Have you resisted the Savior's efforts to shape and form you? If so, where does fear play a role in that resistance?

Sometimes the Archer Waits to Use Us

Secret weapons aren't used in every instance. If they were, they wouldn't be secret.

I can become impatient waiting in the quiver. Sometimes I think I know best and peek my head out, shouting my own thoughts. This method always seems to backfire. Trusting the Archer's timing has consistently proven to be the better route, despite what I might think.

I recently heard a phrase that went something like this: there's nothing more irrelevant than the score at halftime. Our lives are still unfolding.

So often, it feels like I need to *do* something. But more often, the answer is to let go and give the situation to God. This is usually counterintuitive to what I think should happen. However, if I don't let go and get out of the Savior's way, the person I am trying to save might never reach rock bottom. The Savior *is* the rock at the bottom.

During such times, I am trying my best to save the struggling person. Desperately reaching for them. Grasping at them. Running after them. Begging them.

The actual answer is often to do the unthinkable: nothing. That's because Christ can do things that I simply can't if I step out of His way. He is the Savior, and I cannot fill His role.

Of course, sometimes action is necessary. Sometimes I get to be the arrow.

How can someone tell the difference? The only one who really knows the answer to that question is the Archer. As arrows in the quiver, we can definitely ask Him if and when it's time to come out for His special purposes.

He knows. His timing is perfect. Trust Him.

Who Women Are to God

Sometimes we underestimate our roles and value as women. It's easy to internalize destructive and untrue messages about who we are judged to be, and about our worth being considered as less than that of others.

These messages are not true. Satan is lying to us. He attacks women with great effort because, as Sheri Dew said, "[Satan] knows that those who rock the cradle can rock his earthly empire."[52]

Women are not second-class citizens in the kingdom of God. Many things testify of our great worth, and one of the greatest is that Heavenly Father has chosen to be a co-creator with us. Also, President Gordon B. Hinckley said, "Then came the creation of man, and culminating that act of divinity came the crowning act, the creation of woman."[53]

When women grow in worth as daughters of God, we stand out in stunning ways. We sound different, our countenances shine, and we don't puff up but neither do we shrink. As we grow in divine worth, we develop a deep love for people, and we gain the capacity to stand in truth without being disagreeable.

I realize that it can feel like we are simply placeholders at times, but *God does not see us this way*. We do not need to be timid about performing our duties or regarding speaking out as directed by the Spirit.

President Nelson taught, "As a righteous, endowed Latter-day Saint woman, you speak and teach with power and authority from God. Whether by exhortation or conversation, we need your voice teaching the doctrine of Christ. We need your input in family, ward, and stake councils. Your participation is essential and never ornamental!"[54]

We are needed, wanted by God, and rightful heirs of His kingdom. We need not shrink if others do not see us in this light. When we believe God over men, we let God prevail in our lives.

President Nelson said, "We, your brethren, need your strength, your conversion, your conviction, your ability to lead, your wisdom, and your voices. The kingdom of God is not and cannot be complete without women

---

52. Sheri Dew, "Are We Not All Mothers?," *Ensign*, Nov. 2001, 96.
53. Gordon B. Hinckley, "Women of the Church," *Ensign*, Nov. 1996, 67.
54. Russell M. Nelson, "Spiritual Treasures," *Ensign* or *Liahona*, May 2019, 79.

who make sacred covenants and then keep them, women who can speak with the power and authority of God!"[55]

Sister in Zion, daughter of the Most High God, and heir to eternity—step forward in the humble assurance that you *are* of great worth. You are wanted and needed in His kingdom in heaven *and* on the earth. You are irreplaceable. After all, heaven broke the mold after you were dreamed up and created.

Thanks for walking this journey with me. I love you dearly. —Jeni

---

55. Russell M. Nelson, "A Plea to My Sisters," *Ensign* or *Liahona*, Nov. 2015, 96.

Epilogue

I AM A BELIEVER IN FAIRY TALES. "HAPPILY EVER AFTERS" ARE DEFINITELY my thing.

And I also believe that if current circumstances are less than ideal, our stories must not be finished yet.

I am living in an unfinished story right now, and I am not yet sure how it will end. I can say that my current circumstances are more of a nightmare variety. My soul feels crushed, and I find myself relating to the Lord of the vineyard from Jacob 5 as I ask, "What more could I have done?" I am grieving with Christ over things that could have been but aren't.

Some of the most beautiful marriages have been made from the ashes of sex addiction, and I have always hoped that would be the case for me as well. But it doesn't look like redemption will happen in my current marriage, and I am heartbroken.

Also, though, I believe that Christ delights in penning some stunning stories, and I believe that my own story will eventually have an ending that will be amazing! It just isn't finished yet.

After all, Christ is the *Redeemer*. He will redeem my broken heart, and someday I will find great joy in these hard trials that formed my character and led to eternal destinies.

Today, though, I am grieving and am finding solace that my Savior has been running to me with that succor only He can provide. He's such a good God, and I adore Him.

I adore you too, dear friend. Thanks for throwing buckets of water on the flames of betrayal by just being here and being you.

Love,
Jeni

About the Author

Jeni Brockbank lives with her six children in Northern Utah where she is a betrayal coach and a podcaster. She delights in applying the gospel of Jesus Christ to everyday life. She loves to float on lazy rivers, snuggle her children, and have long lunches with amazing friends. Jeni loves the color red because it reminds her that she is individually important to her Heavenly Father.

Scan to visit

https://healinginchristslight.com/